THE MINISTER'S
SERVICE
HANDBOOK

BY JAMES L. CHRISTENSEN

FLEMING H. REVELL COMPANY

Except where marked otherwise, Scripture quotations in this volume are from the *Revised Standard Version of the Bible*, copyrighted 1946 and 1952 by the Division of Christian Education, National Council of Churches, and used by permission.

Scripture quoted from *The New Testament in Modern English* by J. B. Phillips, copyrighted 1959, is used with the permission of The Macmillan Company.

Acknowledgment is made to the following, who have granted permission for the reprinting of copyrighted material:

BOOSEY & HAWKES, INC. for the words of "Bless This House" by Helen Taylor. Copyright 1928, 1932 by Boosey & Hawkes; renewed 1956 and printed by permission of the copyright owners.

HARPER & BROTHERS for excerpt from *Arrows of Light* by Boynton Merrill, copyright 1935; for material from *The Daily Altar* by Willett and Morrison, copyright 1918.

ALFRED A. KNOPF, INC. for material reprinted from *The Prophet* by Kahlil Gibran with permission of the publisher, Alfred A. Knopf, Inc. Copyright 1923 by Kahlil Gibran; renewal copyright 1951 by Administrators C. T. A. of Kahlil Gibran Estate, and Mary G. Gibran.

THE MACMILLAN COMPANY for selections from *The Art of Ministering to the Sick* by Richard C. Cabot and Russell L. Dick, copyright 1936 by The Macmillan Company.

CHARLES SCRIBNER'S SONS for prayer from *Prayers for Services* edited by Morgan Phelps Noyes, copyright 1934 Charles Scribner's Sons and reprinted with their permission.

THE WESTMINSTER PRESS for material from *The Book of Common Worship*. Copyright 1946 by The Board of Christian Education of the Presbyterian Church in the U. S. A. Used by permission.

Additional acknowledgments are included in the chapter notes.

To Dr. G. Edwin Osborn, my seminary professor, whose influence upon my ministry has grown more profound with the passing of every year

Contents

5

SECTION EIGHT: THE FUNERAL

SECTION NINE: HOSPITAL VISITATION

Upon Entering the Hospital, Before an Operation, Birth of a Baby, One Handicapped, One Convalescing, On Forgiveness, When Morale Is Low, Extreme Illness

For Rest, For Sleep, For Companionship of the Spirit, For Understanding, For Patience to Overcome Handicap, To Accept Pain, Before an Operation, With One Beyond Healing, With One Mentally Ill, With a Sick Child, In the Evening, General Prayers for the Sick, At the Time of Death

Confidence in God, God as My Fortress, The Eternity of God, My Strength Cometh from God, Release from Worry, Forget Today's Concern, Ask and Receive, Unto the Weary and Contrite, On Faith

I. Pre-worship Prayers

FOR THE MINISTER

O God, my Heavenly Father, who hast called me to present Thy saving gospel to men: Bless my preparation made for this hour. Forgive my failings, my lack of perception, my inconsistencies, my inadequacies, my neglect. Fill me now with Thy Holy Spirit. As I surrender myself to Thee, take Thou my voice and speak Thy pleading; take Thou my soul and make it a channel of Thy healing grace; take Thou my body and use it as an instrument of Thy will, to the honor of Jesus Christ, whose I am and whom I serve. Amen.

O Thou who hast placed Thy precious treasure in earthen vessels: Humble my spirit before Thee now with a vision of the magnitude of my task which is too great for me, and with a sense of unworthiness to represent Thee, and an utter dependence upon Thy grace and Holy Spirit. May all that I say and do now be done for Thy glory, not mine. May Thy love be communicated in words that will bring light to the confused, healing to the sorrowful, a quickened conscience to the comfortable, salvation to the lost, and the challenge of Jesus Christ to all. Amen.

O Lord, my God, Thou hast set me before Thine altar to lead Thy people in their worship of Thee. Endow me with the sensibilities of an artist and the holiness of a saint that I may fitly bear to Thee the petitions of Thy people and may unerringly direct their minds and hearts into Thy presence.

Thou hast called me to be their spiritual shepherd. May their spiritual well-being be my chief concern. Fill my heart with love for each one. Give me the zeal and unselfish devotion to serve them in their joys and sorrows, in their hopes and fears, in their failures and successes.

Grant me, O Lord, if my study and dedication and spirit merit it, a clearer understanding of the way of man and society, and new revelations of Thy will for Thy people and Thy Kingdom. Then give me the courage of a prophet to declare without compromise, yet in love, the way, the truth, and the life, even Jesus Christ in all His majesty. Amen.[1]

O Christ, grant that my mind may be likened unto Thy mind, and my spirit likened unto Thy Spirit; make me an instrument of Thy peace; where there is hatred, let me sow love; where there is injury, let me pardon; where there is discord, bring union; doubt, faith; despair, hope; darkness, light; sadness, joy.

Grant that I may not seek so much to be consoled as to console; to be understood as to understand; to be loved, as to love; for it is in giving that we receive; it is in pardoning that we are forgiven; and it is in dying to sin that we are born to life abundant and eternal. Amen.[2]

FOR THE ORGANIST AND CHOIR

O God of beauty and harmony, in whose presence the heavenly choirs chant their chorales, and harps and trumpets resound as the voice of many waters: We thank Thee for the organ and the one whom Thou hast endowed with ability to play upon it. Guide *her* to appropriate selections that will honor Thee; bless *her* with a spirit of reverence and an alertness in mind. Direct *her* fingers to notes and chords that will swell to praise Thee and Thy Son Jesus Christ, in whom is perfect concord. Amen.

O Thou, who art worthy of careful and sincere worship, and who hast appointed us to lead Thy people in adoration of Thee: Accept our ministry of music in this hallowed place of prayer. May Thy people be moved to join, with understanding, in the songs of praise, and as they listen to the harmonies of the instrument and choir may they be influenced to holy and heavenly thoughts. Amen.

O Thou who dost unlock the doors of the soul through the medium of music, and who speaks courage and peace to our hearts through songs: Bless with Thy spirit the voices of those who sing Thy message. Make Thy light to shine from their faces and Thy love to glow within their hearts, so that all who worship here may see the beauty of Thy holiness through Jesus Christ, our Lord.

Open Thou our lips, O Lord, and our mouths shall sing forth Thy praise. Attune our hearts unto Thee that we might worship Thee in spirit and in truth. Amen.

FOR OTHERS WHO ASSIST

USHERS

For the privilege of service in this sacred and holy place, we pause to thank Thee. Help us now to be reverent in spirit and attentive to our task. Give to us an understanding of the holiness of worship and make us sensitive to the needs of Thy people. Guard us from disrespectful actions and from wandering thoughts. May all that we do be acceptable to Thee, through Jesus Christ our Lord. Amen.

THOSE RECEIVING THE OFFERING

As we receive and present to Thee the tithes and offerings of Thy children, grant that our own bodies, souls, minds, and spirits may be for Thee living sacrifices, holy and acceptable in Thy sight, through Jesus Christ our Lord. Amen.

O Lord, who art constantly adored, grant us an appreciative spirit, a dignified manner, a quiet confidence, and a sense of sacredness as we bring to Thine altar in behalf of these people their gifts of love and symbols of consecration, for Jesus' sake. Amen.

FOR THOSE CONDUCTING THE LORD'S SUPPER

Forbid us, O Lord, to take lightly this responsibility. As we handle these emblems representing our Saviour's broken body and shed blood, make us aware that this is holy ground. May nothing in our attitude, manner, or procedure interfere with the worshipers discerning the values unseen. As we assist others in their Holy Communion, may we likewise commune with Thee in spirit and in truth, through Jesus Christ our Lord. Amen.

II. Call to Worship Sentences, Invocation Prayers, and Benedictions

GENERAL CALL TO WORSHIP SENTENCES

Whosoever thou art that enterest this church, be silent, be thoughtful, be reverent, for this is none other than the House of God.

To worship is to quicken the conscience by the holiness of God, to feed the mind with the truth of God, to purge the imagination by the beauty of God, to open the heart to the love of God, to devote the will to the purpose of God.[1]

You who through worship would find God, know ye not that God this very hour is seeking you? Lay before Him now a mind open to all truth, a spirit attuned to the whisper of the still small voice, a heart responsive to the cries of human needs, and a will committed to the walking of His way: then you shall go forth a soul renewed, exalted, ennobled, empowered, for our Great God is a Giver Supreme.[2]

To all who mourn and need comfort, to all who are weary and need rest, to all who are friendless and wish friendship, to all who pray and to all who do not but should, to all who sin and need a Saviour, and to whomsoever will, this church opens wide the door and in the name of Jesus bids you welcome.

Be still, and know that I am God. I am exalted among the nations, I am exalted in the earth (*Psalm 46:10*).

My soul longs, yea, faints for the courts of the Lord; my heart and flesh sing for joy to the living God (*Psalm 84:2*).

Wait for the Lord; be strong, and let your heart take courage; yea, wait for the Lord (*Psalm 27:14*).

O come, let us worship and bow down, let us kneel before the Lord, our Maker. For he is our God, and we are the people of his pasture, and the sheep of his hand (*Psalm 95:6-7*).

Extol the Lord our God, and worship at his holy mountain; for the Lord our God is holy (*Psalm 99:9*).

Serve the Lord with gladness! Come into his presence with singing! Enter his gates with thanksgiving, and his courts with praise! Give thanks to him, bless his name! For the Lord is good; his steadfast love endures for ever, and his faithfulness to all generations (*Psalm 100:2, 4-5*).

This is the day which the Lord has made; let us rejoice and be glad in it (*Psalm 118:24*).

I lift up mine eyes to the hills. From whence does my help come? My help comes from the Lord, who made heaven and earth (*Psalm 121:1-2*).

I was glad when they said to me, "Let us go to the house of the Lord!" (*Psalm 122:1*).

Our help is in the name of the Lord, who made heaven and earth. The Lord is near to all who call upon him, to all who call upon him in truth (*Psalms 124:8; 145:18*).

Seek the Lord while he may be found, call upon him while he is near; let the wicked forsake his way, and the unrighteous man his thoughts; let him return to the Lord, that he may have mercy on him; and to our God, for he will abundantly pardon (*Isaiah 55:6-7*).

The Lord is in his holy temple; let all the earth keep silence before him (*Habakkuk 2:20*).

Your Father knows what you need before you ask him. But seek first his kingdom and his righteousness, and all these things shall be yours as well (*Matthew 6:8, 33*).

Draw near to God and he will draw near to you (*James 4:8*).

Ask, and it will be given you; seek and you will find; knock, and it will be opened to you (*Matthew 7:7*).

Come to me, all who labor and are heavy-laden, and I will give you rest. Take my yoke upon you, and learn from me; for I am gentle and lowly in heart, and you will find rest for your souls (*Matthew 11:28-29*).

The hour is coming, and now is, when the true worshipers will worship the Father in spirit and truth, for such the Father seeks to worship him. God is spirit, and those who worship him must worship him in spirit and truth (*John 4:23-24*).

GENERAL INVOCATIONS

Almighty God, unto whom all hearts are open, all desires known, and from whom no secrets are hid; Cleanse the thoughts of our hearts by the inspiration of thy Holy Spirit, that we may perfectly love thee, and worthily magnify thy holy Name; through Christ our Lord. Amen.[3]

O Thou in whom we live and move and have our being; we offer and present to Thee our souls and our bodies, our thoughts and our desires, our words and our deeds, to be a living and continual sacrifice; through Jesus Christ our Lord. Amen.[4]

Author of the world's joy, bearer of the earth's pain, friend of the thankful, counselor of the weak, hope of the aged, inspirer of the young: We dedicate to Thee our worship, and pray that Thou wilt replenish the reservoirs of our souls with Thy power and love. Amen.

Eternal God, who are beyond all our thoughts about Thee, higher than all the words we speak concerning Thee, and greater than all we confine in our emotions about Thee: We stand at attention to acknowledge Thee, and bow in humility to thank Thee, in the name of Jesus Christ by whom we know Thee. Amen.

Like ships storm-driven into port, like wanderers begging refuge from the darkness of night, like starving souls seeking living bread, like flowers turning to the sun, like prodigals seeking the father when all is spent: So we come to Thee seeking hope after fear, calm after storm, and rest

after work. Satisfy our deeper longings with Thy presence
and peace. Amen.

O Thou from whom, in whom, and for whom we are:
We thank Thee that Thou hast made the world and us so
that we cannot escape Thee and that Thou comest to us
through every channel of expression, even though at times
our reception is blurred with interference. Penetrate our de-
lusions, shine through our spiritual deafness, interpret to
us Thyself so that we may know Thee. Amen.

God our Father, the citadel of our thoughts, the foundation of our character, and the spring from which comes
the water of life: We come to acknowledge Thee, to think
Thy thoughts after Thee, to expose our souls to Thee, and
to seek refreshment of spirit from Thee. Amen.

Almighty God, Thou has promised power to those whose
lives are attuned to Thee: From the noisy, demanding
ways of the business world to the calm of this sanctuary
dedicated to the life of the soul, we have come to gaze
upon Thee and to recharge our sagging spirits. Amen.

Lord God, on this day which Thou hast ordained for
worship and rest: We come to rest not only from the routine
of work, but also from selfish cares, overweening ambitions,
the memory of stings, from groundless fears, and burden-
some sins, in order that we may be completely refreshed
through Jesus Christ. Amen.

God almighty and eternal, whose greatness demands our
highest praise, and whose love deserves our most costly
sacrifice: We now prepare our thoughts and hearts that we

might worship Thee in spirit and truth and worthily magnify Thy holy name. Amen.

Heavenly Father of all that is, the ground of our being, the breath of our life, the source of the morality which sustains men, the security amid the changes of this mortal life: That which is deepest in us reaches out in gratitude to Thee, through Jesus Christ. Amen.

O God, how great Thou art; how small we are. How infinite is Thy wisdom; how limited is ours. How everlasting Thou art; how brief our span. How high and good are Thy ways; how selfish and impure are ours. Touch us again with Thy transforming power. Amen.

O Christ of God, eye of our seeing, truth of our speaking, heart of our loving: We bow in adoration of Thee. Amen.

Eternal Father, the quest of the ages, long sought, often doubted, yet in the fullness of time revealed in Jesus the Christ: We humble ourselves before Thee. We experience Thy presence in the impulse toward forgiveness after we have wronged ones we love. We know Thee in the mercy that has melted our hearts in the face of pain and suffering. The aspirations which challenge and motivate us to noble actions are but the visit of Thy Spirit to our life. Amen.

O Lord our God, giver of all true thoughts, rewarder of those who diligently seek Thee, the life of all, and the hope of the distressed: Accept now the thanksgiving, contrition, sacrifice, and repentance of our worship that out of Thy mercy we may be renewed in spirit and service through Jesus Christ. Amen.

O Thou who art found by those who truly seek Thee, known by those who love, and seen by those whose hearts are pure: Let us feel Thy presence in this sacred place. We bring to Thee the thirst we cannot quench at any earthly spring, and the hunger which alone is satisfied by Thy Word. Withdrawn in this place from the turmoil of the world, send us a blessing from above that will lift us out of fear into faith, and out of foolish ways into Thy ways. Amen.

Gracious Father, whose mercy is higher than the heavens, wider than our wanderings, and deeper than our sins: We have come to this solemn and sacred place to worship Thee. May the meaning of this cause us to go forth with strength, to walk in uprightness, to glorify Thee through Jesus Christ. Amen.

O Thou who art the light of the minds that know Thee, the life of the souls that love Thee, the strength of the hearts that serve Thee: Bless this service with Thy Spirit so that the visions of Thy holiness seen here, the truth presented here, the responsibilities realized here, and the covenants entered into here may linger on to glorify Thee through Jesus Christ. Amen.

EVENING CALL TO WORSHIP
SENTENCES AND INVOCATIONS

Call to Worship: Cast your burden on the Lord, and he will sustain you; he will never permit the righteous to be moved (*Psalm 55:22*).

Invocation: O God, shepherd of Thy people, who does neither slumber nor sleep: In the quiet of this sanctuary we bring our hearts with their unuttered yearnings. Thou who seest in secret, minister to each of us in silence, as we wait before Thee. Amen.

Call to Worship: He who dwells in the shelter of the Most High, who abides in the shadow of the Almighty, will say to the Lord, "My refuge and my fortress; my God, in whom I trust" (*Psalm 91:1-2*).

Invocation: Lord of the evening hour, as the darkness of night settles upon the earth filling the glens and valleys with peace, so may Thy Holy Spirit pervade the secret places of our lives to give us the security of Thy never-failing love. Amen.

Call to Worship: And there shall be continuous day (it is known to the Lord), not day and not night, for at evening time there shall be light (*Zechariah 14:7*).

Invocation: O Thou before whose eyes all human hearts lie bare and open, forbid that we should seek to hide from Thee anything that we have done or thought or imagined. What is hidden from the knowledge of others, let us now acknowledge to Thee. Let the light of Thy countenance illumine the darkness of our ignorance and folly, of our sorrow and sin, that we may be quickened and refreshed in spirit through the nightly ministry of Thy healing power. Amen.

BENEDICTIONS

The Lord bless you and keep you: The Lord make his face to shine upon you, and be gracious to you: The Lord lift up his countenance upon you, and give you peace. Amen (*Numbers 6:24-26*).

Grace [be] to you and peace from God our Father and the Lord Jesus Christ (*I Corinthians 1:3*).

And the peace of God, which passes all understanding, will keep your hearts and your minds in Christ Jesus (*Philippians 4:7*).

The grace of the Lord Jesus Christ and the love of God and the fellowship of the Holy Spirit be with you all (*II Corinthians 13:14*).

Now to him who by the power at work within us is able to do far more abundantly than all that we ask or think, to him be glory in the church and in Christ Jesus to all generations, for ever and ever. Amen (*Ephesians 3:20, 21*).

Now to him who is able to keep you from falling and to present you without blemish before the presence of his glory with rejoicing, to the only God, our Savior through Jesus Christ our Lord, be glory, majesty, dominion, and authority, before all time and now and for ever. Amen (*Jude 1:24, 25*).

III. The Offering

OFFERTORY SENTENCES AND PRAYERS

Offer to God a sacrifice of thanksgiving, and pay your vows to the Most High (*Psalm 50:14*).

As our expression of gratitude to Thee for Thy love and goodness to us, our Father, we would not bring that which costs us nothing, but that which represents sacrifice and self-denying love, in the name of Jesus Christ. Amen.

Honor and majesty are before him; strength and beauty are in his sanctuary. Ascribe to the Lord, O families of the peoples, ascribe to the Lord glory and strength! Ascribe to the Lord the glory due his name; bring an offering, and come into his courts (*Psalm 96:6-8*).

O Lord, Thou has blessed us far beyond our deserving or ability to understand. We present now, in humility and thankfulness, our tokens of gratitude for Thy tender mercies, and dedicate them to Thy Kingdom's work, through Jesus Christ our Lord. Amen.

Bring the full tithes into the storehouse, that there may be food in my house; and thereby put me to the test, says the Lord of hosts, if I will not open the windows of heaven for you and pour down for you an overflowing blessing (*Malachi 3:10*).

O Lord, who hast redeemed us with a costly sacrifice of blood: May we not offer Thee the leftover of Thy bounty to us, but rather a sacred portion in respect to Thine ownership of all and to demonstrate our earnestness for the sake of Jesus Christ. Amen.

Moreover it is required of stewards that they be found trustworthy (*I Corinthians 4:2*).

We humble ourselves in recognition, O God, that Thou art the eternal owner of all that there is, and all that we have. Thou hast entrusted to our management a small amount of time, talent, and possessions. Grant us the character and the unselfishness to administer these commodities as Thou wouldst have us do. As Thou hast been faithful in providing for us, may we be faithful in our responsibilities to Thee, we ask in the name of Jesus. Amen.

On the first day of every week, each of you is to put something aside and store it up, as he may prosper (*I Corinthians 16:2*).

O Thou, whose mercies are new with every morning, and who hast preserved our lives through another week: We come now to acknowledge by our offerings Thy goodness, and to use loyally this opportunity to honor Thy holy name, through Jesus Christ. Amen.

Do not lay up for yourselves treasures on earth, where moth and rust consume and where thieves break in and steal, but lay up for yourselves treasures in heaven, where neither moth nor rust consumes and where thieves do not break in and steal. For where your treasure is, there will your heart be also (*Matthew 6:19-21*).

O Thou whose ways are higher than our ways: Help us so to use our temporal commodities to exchange for a quality of spirit that we shall merit a wealth of spiritual grace and a blessed eternal inheritance, through Jesus Christ, our Lord. Amen.

He who is faithful in a very little is faithful also in much; and he who is dishonest in a very little is dishonest also in much (*Luke 16:10*).

Dear Father in Heaven: May our gifts be acceptable to Thee. Sanctify the gift and consecrate the giver and glorify Thine own name through our humble service on the earth, we pray for Jesus' sake. Amen.[1]

What shall I render to the Lord for all his bounty to me? I will lift up the cup of salvation and call on the name of the Lord, I will pay my vows to the Lord in the presence of all his people (*Psalm 116:12-14*).

Not of our deserving but of Thy mercy, Thou hast endowed us with treasures. Forgive us for acting as though our ease, comfort, and wealth has been of our own making. Amen.

Offer right sacrifices, and put your trust in the Lord (*Psalm 4:5*).

Curb our material desires, O Lord, and give us the willingness as Thy disciples to assume a simpler standard of life, thus to release more wealth for advancing Thy Kingdom on earth. Amen.

Now as you excel in everything—in faith, in utterance, in knowledge, in all earnestness, and in your love for us— see that you excel in this gracious work also (*II Corinthians 8:7*).

O Lord, in these complex and confused times, give us intellectual insight, depth of conviction, and closeness to Thee that we may follow our Master's path of sacrifice and selfless service, and thus help quench the world's thirst for personal Christian love. Amen.

For what will it profit a man, if he gains the whole world and forfeits his life? Or what shall a man give in return for his life? (*Matthew 16:26*).

Forbid, Lord, that we should set our hearts so much on earthly riches that we neglect the true wealth of our soul. When Thou seest that our possessions are a hindrance to the progress of our souls and a peril to our salvation, then remove them from us and give them to those who can more wisely use them; or help us to have the discipline and spiritual perspective to be rich in good works, humble-minded and willing to distribute to the needs of others. Thus, may our stewardship honor Thee, in the name of Jesus Christ. Amen.

No servant can serve two masters; for either he will hate the one and love the other, or he will be devoted to the one and despise the other. You cannot serve God and mammon (*Luke 16:13*).

O Thou by whose wisdom and grace we have been privileged to live: In humility and gratitude we bring Thee what is Thine. Enable us, with our offerings, to present ourselves as living sacrifices to do Thy will, through Jesus Christ our Lord. Amen.

And he said to them, "Go into all the world and preach the gospel to the whole creation. He who believes and is baptized will be saved; but he who does not believe will be condemned" (*Mark 16:15-16*).

God and Father of mankind, who dost have the ultimate claim upon our lives, illumine us with the significance of the great commission, compel us with the urgency of the task, and grant us the dedication to do our part in spreading Thy gospel over all the earth, to the end that men, everywhere, may know Thee through Jesus Christ. Amen.

Take heed what you hear; the measure you give will be the measure you get, and still more will be given you (*Mark 4:24*).

Dear Lord, forgive us for confusing our material wants with our actual needs, and for those of us who have so much, for thoughtlessly forgetting those who have so little. Amen.

Honor the Lord with your substance and with the first fruits of all your produce (*Proverbs 3:9*).

Holy and majestic God, may the gifts we bring now be worthy to present to Thee without shame, hiding, or excuse, and may we, the givers, be found acceptable in Thy sight, through Jesus Christ, the Lord. Amen.

Take heed, and beware of all covetousness; for a man's life does not consist in the abundance of his possessions (*Luke 12:15*).

O Thou to whom belong the earth and the fulness thereof, and who has committed to our care a goodly portion of possessions: Help us to realize that our ownership is not absolute nor eternal. Give us the wisdom and desire to use the means in our possession so as to honor Thy name and to bless humanity. Amen.

But seek first his kingdom and his righteousness, and all these things shall be yours as well (*Matthew 6:33*).

In these moments, our Father, help us to see that "enough to live on" is always less than we want, and is less than we have. Give us a great concern about what to live for; then, as Thou hast promised, we shall have enough to live on. Amen.

Each one must do as he has made up his mind, not reluctantly or under compulsion, for God loves a cheerful giver (*II Corinthians 9:7*).

O God, we have been bought with a price, and stand before Thee, eternally in debt. We lay upon Thine altar these joyful sacrifices in appreciation of the privilege of being counted among Christ's followers. Amen.

And he said to all, "If any man would come after me, let him deny himself and take up his cross daily and follow me" (*Luke 9:23*).

Forbid, O God, that we should forget, amid our earthly comforts, the pains of betrayal, lonely agony, false accusations, broken heart, and torturous death that our Lord Jesus endured for our salvation. As Thou didst give Thyself utterly for us, may we give ourselves entirely to Thee. Amen.

IV.   Communion, or The Lord's Supper

INVITATIONS TO COMMUNION AND PRAYER

It is written, man shall not live by bread alone, but by every word that proceeds from the mouth of God (*Matthew 4:4*).

Blessed are those who hunger and thirst for righteousness, for they shall be satisfied (*Matthew 5:6*).

"I am the living bread which came down from heaven; if any one eats of this bread, he will live for ever; and the bread which I shall give for the life of the world is my flesh." . . . So Jesus said to them, "Truly, truly, I say to you, unless you eat the flesh of the Son of man and drink his blood, you have no life in you; he who eats my flesh and drinks my blood has eternal life, and I will raise him up at the last day. For my flesh is food indeed, and my blood is drink indeed. He who eats my flesh and drinks my blood abides in me, and I in him" (*John 6:51, 53-56*).

They who wait for the Lord shall renew their strength, they shall mount up with wings like eagles, they shall run and not be weary, they shall walk and not faint (*Isaiah 40:31*).

Whoever drinks of the water that I shall give him will never thirst; the water that I shall give him will become in him a spring of water welling up to eternal life. . . . Let him who is thirsty come, let him who desires take the water of life without price (*John 4:14; Revelation 22:17b*).

Come to me, all who labor and are heavy-laden, and I will give you rest. Take my yoke upon you, and learn from me; for I am gentle and lowly in heart, and you will find rest for your souls. For my yoke is easy, and my burden is light (*Matthew 11:28-30*).

Cleanse out the old leaven that you may be fresh dough, as you really are unleavened. For Christ, our paschal lamb, has been sacrificed. Let us, therefore, celebrate the festival, not with the old leaven, the leaven of malice and evil, but with the unleavened bread of sincerity and truth (*I Corinthians 5:7-8*).

For just as the body is one and has many members, and all the members of the body, though many, are one body, so it is with Christ. For by one Spirit we were all baptized into one body—Jews or Greeks, slaves or free—and all were made to drink of one Spirit. . . . Now you are the body of Christ and individually members of it (*I Corinthians 12:12, 13, 27*).

Behold, I stand at the door and knock; if any one hears my voice and opens the door, I will come in to him and eat with him, and he with me (*Revelation 3:20*).

I appeal to you therefore, brethren, by the mercies of God, to present your bodies as a living sacrifice, holy and acceptable to God, which is your spiritual worship (*Romans 12:1*).

On the first day of the week . . . we were gathered together to break bread. . . . And they devoted themselves to the apostles' teaching and fellowship, to the breaking of bread and the prayers (*Acts 20:7a; Acts 2:42*).

And as Moses lifted up the serpent in the wilderness, so must the Son of man be lifted up, that whoever believes in him may have eternal life. For God so loved the world that he gave his only Son, that whoever believes in him should not perish but have eternal life (*John 3:14-16*).

I am the true vine, and my Father is the vinedresser. . . . Abide in me, and I in you. As the branch cannot bear fruit by itself, unless it abides in the vine, neither can you, unless you abide in me. I am the vine, you are the branches. He who abides in me, and I in him, he it is that bears much fruit, for apart from me you can do nothing. . . . By this my Father is glorified, that you bear much fruit, and so prove to be my disciples (*John 15:1, 4, 5, 8*).

If we walk in the light, as he is in the light, we have fellowship with one another, and the blood of Jesus his Son cleanses us from all sin (*I John 1:7*).

Greater love has no man than this, that a man lay down his life for his friends. . . . But God shows his love for us in that while we were yet sinners Christ died for us (*John 15:13; Romans 5:8*).

Therefore, since we are justified by faith, we have peace with God through our Lord Jesus Christ (*Romans 5:1*).

Who shall separate us from the love of Christ? Shall tribulation, or distress, or persecution, or famine, or nakedness, or peril, or sword? . . . No, in all these things we are more than conquerors through him who loved us. For I am sure that neither death, nor life, nor angels, nor principalities, nor things present, nor things to come, nor powers, nor height, nor depth, nor anything else in all creation, will be able to separate us from the love of God in Christ Jesus our Lord (*Romans 8:35, 37-39*).

A new commandment I give to you, that you love one another; even as I have loved you, that you also love one another. By this all men will know that you are my disciples, if you have love for one another (*John 13:34, 35*).

For where two or three are gathered in my name, there am I in the midst of them (*Matthew 18:20*).

Ye who do truly and earnestly repent of your sins, and are in love and charity with your neighbors, and intend to lead a new life, following the commandments of God, and walking from henceforth in His holy ways: draw near with reverence, faith, and thanksgiving, and take the Supper of the Lord to your comfort.[1]

Come to this table, not because you must but because you may; come to testify not that you are righteous but that you sincerely love our Lord Jesus Christ and desire to be His true disciples. Come, not because you are strong, but because you are weak; not because you have any claim on heaven's rewards, but because in your frailty and sin you stand in constant need of heaven's mercy and help; come, not to express an opinion, but to seek a Presence and to pray for a Spirit. And now that the Supper of the Lord is spread before you, lift up your minds and hearts above all selfish fears and cares. Let this bread and this cup be to you the witness and signs of the grace of our Lord Jesus Christ, the love of God, and the communion of the Holy Spirit. Before the throne of the heavenly Father and the cross of the Redeemer make your humble confession of sin, consecrate your lives to Christian obedience and service, and pray for strength to do the holy and blessed will of God.[2]

I come, not because I am worthy; not for any righteousness of mine; for I have grievously sinned and fallen short of what, by God's help, I might have been.

I come, not because there is any magic in partaking of the symbols of Christ's body and blood.

I come, not from a sense of duty that is unacquainted with deep appreciation for this blessed means of grace— the highest privilege in Christian worship.

I come, because Christ bids me come. It is His table, and He extends the invitation.

I come because it is a memorial to Him, as often as it is done in remembrance of Him. Here is vivid portrayal of the redeeming sacrifice of the Christ of Calvary. His matchless life, His victorious sufferings, and His faithfulness even unto death, are brought to mind, and I bow humbly before Him and worship.

I come because in contemplation of the Father and His Son our Saviour, I am moved to thanksgiving for so great a salvation.

I come because in this encounter with the Saviour I am made to feel the wrongness of my sins, base desires, unchristian motives, hurtful attitudes, vain ambitions, and the things I have done which I ought not to have done and the things I have failed to do which God expected me to do. I acknowledge my utter unworthiness and walk again the painful, but necessary, path of repentance.

I come because forgiveness comes with true repentance. I arise with the assurance of pardon, rejoicing in the opportunity of a new beginning.

I come because I want to experience high communion with God the Father, revealed in Jesus Christ, and ever present in the Person of the Holy Spirit. And, having fellowship with Him, I am drawn closer to all who kneel with me at the altar and, indeed, I become conscious of my kinship with all men everywhere who claim my Christ as Saviour, the Holy universal fellowship of believers.

I come because I arise from the Lord's table with new strength, courage, poise, and power to live for Him who died for me.[3]

COMMUNION PRAYERS

WORLD-WIDE COMMUNION PRAYER

Almighty and Eternal God, our Heavenly Father, we worship Thee. We thank Thee that Thy love is broad enough to embrace the whole world, yet personal enough to reach out to each believing soul in perfect understanding and redeeming grace.

Within the circle of that love we gather in fellowship with Thy people of every nation and race as members of one Holy Family. Through these symbols of our Saviour's broken body and shed blood, we would all partake of Thy life.

Forgive our littleness of mind and selfishness of spirit which have broken the bonds of Thy family fellowship. Make us all truly one in Christ Jesus. Help us to love one another, as Christ has loved us. Help us also to bear one another's burdens and so fulfill His law.

Even as we sit together at Thy Table and partake of Thy life through Thy presence, make us all truly members of Thy present Body, to be used in fulfilling Thy redemptive purpose in our troubled world. Gathered in our many churches, give us the joy of knowing that we are all united in one Church, the Body of Christ. Amen.[4]

PRAYER OF CONFESSION

O God, whose mercy is from everlasting to everlasting and over all Thy works, we, whom Thou hast brought again to this high and holy hour, give Thee thanks for this fresh opportunity of receiving at Thy bountiful hand and of sharing the fellowship of Thy people; through Jesus Christ our Lord.

We confess that we have been unworthy of the least of Thy gifts. Day after day we have offended against Thee in thought and in word and in deed. We have dishonored Thy name by our carelessness and by our slackness have prevented Thy purposes for ourselves and for others from being fulfilled. We remember promises we failed to keep and vows we failed to fulfill. The excuses we fashioned to hide our faltering loyalty from ourselves cannot hide our faltering loyalty to Thee. We approach Thee not through any merit of our own, but through the merit and mediation of Jesus Christ, Thy Son, our Saviour, who lived and died and rose again for our salvation. For His sake whom Thou hearest always, pardon our offenses, and so perfect Thy strength in our weakness, we pray Thee, that where we have failed we may fail no more. Deliver us from thinking that what we have been we must always be. Remind us, when our hearts condemn us, that Thou art greater than our hearts and canst cleanse us from all unrighteousness, through Jesus Christ our Lord. Amen.[5]

GENERAL COMMUNION PRAYERS

We thank Thee, our Heavenly Father, for this table to which we come, remembering our Lord whose body was broken and whose blood was shed that we may have life. Give us a new vision and a more perfect appreciation of Thine infinite love and mercy. Let these emblems speak to us of redemption from sin and of life eternal which we know through Him whose life, death, and resurrection are represented here. Help us to forget the lesser things that so engross us and help us to fix our attention on that quality of life which is eternal. Give us strength to face temptation, courage to meet any evil that may beset us, and forgiveness for our failures, in Jesus' name. Amen.

Merciful Father, we Thy children assemble in Thy name and in Thy house to break bread and drink of the cup in memory of Thy Son, our Saviour, Jesus Christ. Grant that we may have understanding and humility as we seek to re-enact our Lord's last supper. Hear us as each in his own way seeks personal communion with Thee through Jesus Christ. Amen.[6]

Our Father, who hast been made known to us in Christ, we pray that we may feel Thy presence here today and that Thy spirit and way of life may be real to us. We thank Thee for these emblems of our Lord's broken body and shed blood which remind us that He gave His life that we may see in Him Thy love for us. Help us to know that in Thy love we have grace and mercy through which all our repented sins are forgiven and by which our lives may be transformed with newness. We come before Thee remembering that even as Thou dost love and forgive us, so ought we to love and forgive one another. Strengthen our faith in Christ and help us to be consecrated to His way. Amen.

O God, who canst guide our feet into the sanctuary of Thy presence: Make ready, we beseech Thee, our hearts to receive the sacrament of that love whereby Thy Son hath redeemed us. Amen.

COMMUNION WORDS OF INSTITUTION

For the Bread: Now as they were eating, Jesus took bread and blessed, and broke it, and gave it to the disciples and said, "Take, eat; this is my body."

For the Cup: And he took a cup, and when he had given thanks he gave it to them, saying, "Drink of it, all of you; for this is my blood of the covenant, which is poured out for many for the forgiveness of sins" (*Matthew 26:27, 28*).

For the Bread: The Lord Jesus on the night when he was betrayed took bread, and when he had given thanks, he broke it, and said, "This is my body which is for you. Do this in remembrance of me."

For the Cup: In the same way also the cup, after supper, saying, "This cup is the new covenant in my blood. Do this, as often as you drink it, in remembrance of me" (*I Corinthians 11:23b-25*).

COMMUNION MEDITATIONS

Meet the Living Christ

Create in me a clean heart, O God, and put a new and right spirit within me (*Psalm 51:10*).

When you take the bread in your hand, remind yourself of Him whose body was broken, and do not shun the suffering which still tortures the world by sin, and the sacrifice demanded for its healing.

When you lift this cup to your lips, see the greatness of His spirit whose soul was meek and lowly, pure and committed, and hide not the poverty of your own soul.

Do not desecrate this moment with shallow perception, but through these emblems meet the living Christ.

The Art of Remembering

Do this in remembrance of me (*I Corinthians 11:24*).

Memory is a balancing factor in life. Though we are not to live *in* the past, we do live *by* the past. We keep photographs, mementos, and symbols to remind us of important events, sacrifices made for our heritage, vows we have made, and the love we cherish.

Our Lord did not want to be forgotten. He knew that if faith, morality, love, and proper motivation were to be

kept alive in His disciples, they must remember the purity
of His life, the cost of His sacrifice, and the power of
the resurrection.

So we come to this table today, remembering that here
we may come as near to Calvary as man may come . . .
remembering the "Lamb of God that taketh away the sin
of the world" . . . remembering the great cloud of witnesses
all of whose hands have been on the table and who have
since gone to the "place of many mansions" . . . remembering what we are and what we can become in Christ . . .
remembering that we live not so much to be loved as to
love, not to be served but to serve.

The Table of Brotherhood

The cup of blessing which we bless, is it not a participation in the blood of Christ? The bread which we break, is
it not a participation in the body of Christ? Because there
is one loaf, we who are many are one body, for we all
partake of the same loaf (*I Corinthians 10:16, 17*).

The word "communion" is a translation of the New
Testament word *koinonia*. The followers of Jesus long ago
were bound into a new human fraternity—the church.
It was a new kind of community in which there was inter-
penetration of personality without loss of individuality. It
had supernatural roots derived from God's love in Jesus.
The community life was exhibited and visibly depicted by
the sharing of one loaf and one cup, emblems of the body
of Jesus Christ.

Each communion celebration is a local expression of the
universal church. When Christian hearts respond as one to
Jesus Christ at His Supper, accepting His Lordship, and
pledging allegiance to Him, we find a basis of Christian
brotherhood and unity. We are in Christ as one body, one

church, and one in faith. He is the unseen kinship which binds our hearts in love.

From our divergent views, various backgrounds, separated traditions, and artificial classes, our Lord now invites us to the table of brotherhood, for

> In Christ there is no East or West
> In Him no South or North
> But one great Fellowship of Love
> Throughout the whole wide earth.
>
> In Him shall true hearts everywhere
> Their high communion find. . . .[7]

A Pledge of Loyalty

Now as they were eating, Jesus took bread, and blessed, and broke it, and gave it to the disciples and said, "Take, eat; this is my body." And he took a cup, and when he had given thanks he gave it to them, saying, "Drink of it, all of you; for this is my blood of the covenant, which is poured out for many for the forgiveness of sins (*Matthew 26:26-28*).

The name "breaking of bread," which may be the earliest name for Holy Communion, was familiar in Jewish circles, where most meals had religious overtones. It came from the Oriental home-ritual when the father of the house broke and blessed bread at the beginning of a meal. In that ancient world, to break faith with a man with whom one had broken bread was a most heinous sin. When families or friends were to be separated, this breaking of bread together was a pledge of love and loyalty, even at the sacrifice of body and blood.

To eat and drink at the Lord's table, then, is to bind oneself in loyalty to Christ, to be in love and charity with those with whom one is joined in the Holy Communion, and eventually to be united to all that are good and true. The word "covenant" appears in all the accounts of the institution of the Supper. Whatever else the Lord's Supper is, basically it is a covenant rite, a personal pledge of loyalty, a promise of straight dealing on God's part with us, and our part with Him. As we share in this service, it means we pledge to make all things holy during the following week.

To traduce this vow is to be a traitor to Christ.

Expressing Our Thanks

Greater love has no man than this, that a man lay down his life for his friends (*John 15:13*).

This ceremony has been known in some groups of the Christian tradition as the "Eucharist," meaning "thanksgiving." Jesus "took bread . . . and gave thanks." Indeed, it is a time to recall the mighty acts of God, and to give thanks unto Him.

The background association from which the Lord's Supper emerged was the Passover Feast which the Jewish nation celebrated. As the Jewish Passover celebrated redemption from bondage in Egypt, so the Lord's Supper celebrates the Christians' redemption from the bondage of sin. As the Jewish Passover celebrated the redemption to a new life for Israel under the Law of Moses, so the Lord's Supper celebrates redemption to new life of freedom and liberty for the new Israel under the Law of Christ. As the Jewish Passover celebrated the blessings of God's old covenant under the Law, so the Lord's Supper celebrates the blessings of God's New Covenant under Love. As the Jewish Passover used emblems of unleavened bread and the fruit of the vine to recall the mighty acts of God, so the Lord's Supper uses emblems of bread and the fruit of the vine to represent Christ's broken body and shed blood.

As we recall our deliverance by the power of God in Christ, let us give thanks because "greater love has no man than this, that a man lay down his life for his friends."

A Foretaste of Heaven

For as often as you eat this bread and drink the cup, you proclaim the Lord's death until he comes (*I Corinthians 11:26*).

I tell you I shall not drink again of this fruit of the vine until that day when I drink it new with you in my Father's kingdom (*Matthew 26:29*).

Arnold J. Toynbee, the world's foremost contemporary historian, has written, "The greatest new event in the modern world is still the crucifixion." Think of the magnitude of that statement. The crucifixion in which the whole life of Christ came to focus released the energy that made all the other events possible, and is still the dynamo of our Western civilization.

The Lord's Supper not only looks back to the saving acts of our Lord's life, death, and resurrection; it also looks forward to the consummation of all things. The goal is the Kingdom of God, the rule of God in the hearts of all men. The Kingdom is both *present* and *future*. It is among us now in a limited way; its consummation will be beyond history by God's action. This fellowship with Christ, in the church, is the spearhead of the Kingdom, a foretaste of glory. The Lord expressed His desire that the will of God be done on earth as it is in heaven. It cannot be done so until it is done in us. As we come face to face with the reality of our Lord's sacrificial life and death in this service of communion, may we see the sacrifices we must make.

Guests of the Eternal King

When it was evening, he sat at table with the twelve disciples (*Matthew 26:20*).

A lady who was attempting to get an absentee to attend the regular observance of Holy Communion, closed her appeal by saying, "At every communion a cup is prepared for you which is left untouched."

The communion is a banquet table that is spread with the only bread that will eternally satisfy. There is a place set for everyone in God's family. To eat at the Lord's table is to be the guest of the Eternal King, whose splendor, power and holiness none can ever equal.

To partake of the bread is to be nurtured by the subtle mysteries of the Creator's wisdom, the labor of God, and the work of untold people.

To be privileged to be included at this table is to share in the family of God on earth, to wear the most revered name of all time, and to commune with the Spirit by which the worlds were made.

To drink this cup is to remember Him whose death revealed a glory which no breaking of the body could destroy, no condemnation could degrade, or no sorrow extinguish.

To eat and drink here is the humblest act of life, but it is where your soul is filled with heaven's blessings and made strong with divine forgiveness.

Lord, Is It I?

When it was evening, he sat at table with the twelve disciples; and as they were eating, he said, "Truly, I say

to you, one of you will betray me." And they were very
sorrowful, and began to say to him one after another,
"Is it I, Lord?" (*Matthew 26:20-22*).

The saddest event recorded in Scripture is not what
happened on a hill outside of Jerusalem; it is what happened in the Upper Room. The saddest words of the Bible
are not "and they crucified him," but these, "one of you
shall betray me." The cruelest nails ever driven were not
those driven into the hands and feet of Jesus, but those
His friends drive into His heart.

When the will of Jesus went contrary to the desire of
one of the disciples, he betrayed the Lord for a few worldly
coins. When following Jesus became dangerous, and when
He needed loyal support, His disciples forsook Him and
fled. When an opportunity was given to testify, one who
followed afar off denied Him three times.

It still goes on among His most trusted followers. The
Upper Room question is still appropriate for us to ask
in these quiet moments of introspection. "Lord, is it I?"

What Is an Unworthy Manner?

Whoever, therefore, eats the bread or drinks the cup
of the Lord in an unworthy manner will be guilty of profaning the body and blood of the Lord (*I Corinthians
11:27*).

Is there danger that you and I are not worthy to partake
of the Lord's Supper? Often people refuse to participate,
saying that they are not good enough. The conclusion of
a sensitive conscience should be respected.

However, none deserves what God has done for us.
None is perfect. It is by God's grace that we are forgiven
and justified. And because of this, the Lord invites you

to this table, where you can thank God for His help in making possible whatever good there is in you.

If you have sinned, you can ask God's forgiveness as you determine to live more nearly the life revealed in Christ. If you are perplexed, you can seek God's guidance for the days ahead. If you are in sorrow, you can accept God's peace and comfort. Whatever your need you may come in full trust in God's love.

Only if you are insincere, have no appreciation of the cost of God's love, no reverence for the meaning of these emblems, and no intention of pleasing God—do you partake unworthily. "Let a man examine himself, and so eat of the bread and drink of the cup" (*I Corinthians 11:28*).

Face to Face

Last night I dreamed I saw Him by the laughing waters of Galilee where the multitudes hung breathless on His words; I saw Him break the loaves and fishes and minister to hungry bodies; I saw them spread their garments in the way, and I heard their loud hosannas; I saw the blind go seeing, and the deaf go hearing, and the leper cleansed of his monstrous impurity—yea, I saw the dead come back to life, to think, to speak, to act, to love. And then I saw Him thorn-crowned in Pilate's Judgment Hall; I saw Him go alone to Calvary, deserted by His friends—this Prince of lonely men. I heard His despairing cry, "Why hast Thou forsaken me?" All men fell away from Him— hearts too gross to comprehend, too dull to feel, too frivolous to care. Perhaps had we been there, we would have been as base as they.

Forbid that we should desert Him in the pursuit of life. Forbid that we should hesitate in the face of Christian service. At this sacred table, let us look again into His face and feel again the clasp of His hand—and consecrate ourselves anew.

COMMUNION WITH THE SICK

Opening Sentence: God so loved the world that he gave his only Son, that whoever believes in him should not perish but have eternal life (*John 3:16*).

Invocation: Almighty God, unto whom all hearts are open, all desires known, and from whom no secrets are hid; Cleanse the thoughts of our hearts by the inspiration of thy Holy Spirit, that we may perfectly love thee and worthily magnify thy holy Name. Through Christ our Lord. Amen.

Scripture Reading: The Lord is my shepherd, I shall not want; he makes me lie down in green pastures. He leads me beside still waters; he restores my soul. He leads me in paths of righteousness for his name's sake. Even though I walk through the valley of the shadow of death, I fear no evil; for thou art with me; thy rod and thy staff, they comfort me. Thou preparest a table before me in the presence of my enemies; thou anointest my head with oil, my cup overflows. Surely goodness and mercy shall follow me all the days of my life; and I shall dwell in the house of the Lord for ever (*Psalm 23*).

Communion Meditation: The cup of blessing which we bless, is it not a participation in the blood of Christ? The bread which we break, is it not a participation in the body of Christ? (*I Corinthians 10:16*).

In the broken bread, Christ offered to share with us His life. The Christian who comes to the Lord's table receives a share in the sinless and holy life of Christ which helps to redeem the lives of all. This bread of the Communion service is a means of participation in Christ's body, the church.

Likewise, in the cup Christ offered us a share in His atoning death. When we drink of the cup we declare our readiness to share His sufferings, to shed our blood, and to claim the victory of the eventual departure from this life.

To participate in the death and in the life of Christ is to be identified with the triumph of His resurrection. He gave us fellowship at the most ultimate levels of existence —life and death. Every person has one of each. The emblems symbolize the redemption of life and the redemption of death. As we partake, we are identified with Christ in both.

Prayer of Thanks for the Bread and Cup: Dear Lord and Father of us all: We thank Thee for this bread and cup which remind us of Thy great love for us as expressed in the life, death, and resurrection of Jesus Christ our Saviour. We draw near to Thee in humility and reverence, confessing our sins, knowing that in Thee we will find forgiveness, refuge, hope, and salvation, now and forever. Amen.

Words of Institution for the Bread: And as they were eating, he took bread, and blessed, and broke it, and gave it to them, and said, "Take; this is my body" (*Mark 14:22*).

Words of Institution for the Cup: And he took a cup, and when he had given thanks he gave it to them, and they all drank of it. And he said to them, "This is my blood of the covenant, which is poured out for many" (*Mark 14:23, 24*).

Lord's Prayer in Unison.

Benediction: The Lord bless you and keep you: The Lord make his face to shine upon you, and be gracious to you: The Lord lift up his countenance upon you, and give you peace (*Numbers 6:24-26*).

V.   Reception of New Members and Baptism

RECEPTION OF NEW MEMBERS

PERSON MAKING INITIAL CONFESSION OF FAITH

We read in the word of God: "If you confess with your lips that Jesus is Lord and believe in your heart that God raised him from the dead, you will be saved. For man believes with his heart and so is justified, and he confesses with his lips and so is saved" (*Romans 10:9, 10*).

_____, do you believe that Jesus is the Christ, the Son of the Living God; and do you accept Him as your Lord and Saviour?

Response: I do.

The Lord will bless you in making this good confession, for He has promised, "Every one who acknowledges me before men, I also will acknowledge before my Father who is in heaven; but whoever denies me before men, I also will deny before my Father who is in heaven" (*Matthew 10:32-33*).

PERSON WHO COMES BY LETTER OR STATEMENT
FROM ANOTHER CONGREGATION

Do you publicly declare that you have confessed your faith in our Lord Jesus Christ, and have witnessed to it by being baptized into His name?

Response: I do.

According to the Scripture you have been added by

honour, and keep her in sickness and in health; and, forsaking all others, keep thee only unto her, so long as ye both shall live?

The Man shall answer, I will.

Then shall the Minister say unto the Woman,

_____, wilt thou have this man to thy wedded husband, to live together after God's ordinance in the holy estate of Matrimony? Wilt thou love him, comfort him, honour, and keep him in sickness and in health; and, forsaking all others, keep thee only unto him, so long as ye both shall live?

The Woman shall answer, I will.

Then shall the Minister say, Who giveth this Woman to be married to this Man?

Then shall they give their troth to each other in this manner. The Minister, receiving the Woman at her father's or friend's hands, shall cause the Man with his right hand to take the Woman by her right hand, and to say after him as followeth.

I, _____, take thee, _____, to be my wedded Wife, to have and to hold from this day forward, for better for worse, for richer for poorer, in sickness and in health, to love and to cherish, till death us do part, according to God's holy ordinance; and thereto I plight thee my troth.

Then shall they loose their hands; and the woman with her right hand taking the Man by his right hand, shall likewise say after the Minister,

I, _____, take thee, _____, to my wedded Husband, to have and to hold from this day forward, for better for worse, for richer for poorer, in sickness and in health, to love and to cherish, till death us do part, according to God's holy ordinance; and thereto I give thee my troth.

Then shall they again loose their hands; and the Man

shall give unto the Woman a Ring on this wise: the Minister taking the Ring shall deliver it unto the Man, to put it upon the fourth finger of the Woman's left hand. And the Man holding the Ring there, and taught by the Minister, shall say,

With this Ring I thee wed: In the Name of the Father, and of the Son, and of the Holy Ghost. Amen.

And, before delivering the Ring to the Man, the Minister may say as followeth.

Bless, O Lord, this Ring, that he who gives it and she who wears it may abide in thy peace, and continue in thy favour, unto their life's end; through Jesus Christ our Lord. Amen.

Then, the Man leaving the Ring upon the fourth finger of the Woman's left hand, the Minister shall say,

Let us pray.

Then shall the Minister and the People, still standing, say the Lord's Prayer.

Our Father, who art in heaven, Hallowed be thy name. Thy kingdom come. Thy will be done, On earth as it is in heaven. Give us this day our daily bread. And forgive us our trespasses, As we forgive those who trespass against us. And lead us not into temptation, But deliver us from evil. For thine is the kingdom, and the power, and the glory for ever and ever. Amen.

Then shall the Minister add,

O eternal God, Creator and Preserver of all mankind, Giver of all spiritual grace, the Author of everlasting life; Send thy blessing upon these thy servants, this man and this woman, whom we bless in thy Name; that they, living faithfully together, may surely perform and keep the vow and covenant betwixt them made, (whereof this Ring given and received is a token and pledge), and may ever remain in perfect love and peace together, and live according to thy laws; through Jesus Christ our Lord. Amen.

The Minister may add one or both of the following prayers.

O Almighty God, Creator of mankind, who only art the well-spring of life; Bestow upon these thy servants, if it be thy will, the gift and heritage of children; and grant that they may see their children brought up in thy faith and fear, to the honour and glory of thy Name; through Jesus Christ our Lord. Amen.

O God, who hast so consecrated the state of Matrimony that in it is represented the spiritual marriage and unity betwixt Christ and his Church; Look mercifully upon these thy servants, that they may love, honour, and cherish each other, and so live together in faithfulness and patience, in wisdom and true godliness, that their home may be a haven of blessing and of peace; through the same Jesus Christ our Lord, who liveth and reigneth with thee and the Holy Spirit ever, one God, world without end. Amen.

Then shall the Minister join their right hands together, and say,

Those whom God hath joined together let no man put asunder.

Then shall the Minister speak unto the company.

Forasmuch as _____ and _____ have consented together in holy wedlock, and have witnessed the same before God and this company, and thereto have given and pledged their troth, each to the other, and have declared the same by giving and receiving a Ring, and by joining hands; I pronounce that they are Man and Wife, In the Name of the Father, and of the Son, and of the Holy Ghost. Amen.

The Man and Wife kneeling, the Minister shall add this Blessing.

God the Father, God the Son, God the Holy Ghost, bless, preserve and keep you; the Lord mercifully with his favour look upon you, and fill you with all spiritual benediction and grace; that ye may so live together in this life, that in the world to come ye may have life everlasting. Amen.[2]

ORDER FOR BLESSING OF A CIVIL MARRIAGE

The minister, satisfied that the persons seeking this blessing have been lawfully married, shall say,

Dearly beloved, we are met here in the presence of God to invoke the blessings of the Heavenly Father upon your marriage. Let us reverently bring to remembrance that marriage was instituted by God for the comfort and help of his children and that families might be trained in goodness and godliness of life. Both by his presence and his solemn words Christ honored and sanctioned it; and it is set forth and commended in the Scripture as honorable to all who enter it lawfully, seriously, and with true affection.

The minister then, asking the man to take the right hand of the woman in his right hand shall say,

_____, do you before God and these witnesses acknowledge this woman to be your lawful wedded wife; and do you promise that from this day forward you will be her faithful husband, for better or worse, for richer for poorer, in sickness and in health, to love and to cherish, till death do you part?

The man shall answer, I do.

The minister then, asking the woman to take the right hand of the man in her right hand shall say,

_____, do you before God and these witnesses

acknowledge this man to be your lawful wedded husband; and do you promise that from this day forward you will be his faithful wife, for better for worse, for richer for poorer, in sickness and in health, to love and to cherish till death do you part?

The woman shall answer, I do.

If a ring be provided, the minister upon receiving it shall give it to the man, requesting him, as he places it upon the fourth finger of the woman's left hand to say,

In pledge of the vow made between us, I give thee this ring; in the name of the Father, and of the Son, and of the Holy Spirit. Amen.

Then the minister shall say,

Let us pray. O eternal God, Creator and Preserver of all mankind, Giver of all spiritual grace, the Author of everlasting life: Send thy blessing upon these thy servants, this man and this woman, whom we bless in thy Name; that they, living faithfully together, may surely perform and keep the vow and covenant betwixt them made, and may ever remain in perfect love and peace together, and live according to thy laws, through Jesus Christ our Lord. Amen.

Then the minister and people shall say,

Our Father who art in heaven, hallowed be thy Name. Thy kingdom come. Thy will be done on earth, as it is in heaven. Give us this day our daily bread. And forgive us our debts, as we forgive our debtors. And lead us not into temptation; but deliver us from evil: For thine is the kingdom, and the power, and the glory, for ever. Amen.

The bride and groom kneeling to receive the benediction, the Minister shall say,

God the Father, God the Son, God the Holy Spirit, bless, preserve, and keep you; the Lord mercifully with his favor look upon you, and fill you with all spiritual benediction and grace; that you may so live together in this life, that in the world to come you may have life ever lasting. Amen.[3]

VII.   Dedication Services for Infants and Parents

PUBLIC DEDICATION SERVICE FOR INFANTS AND PARENTS

Scripture

And when the time came for their purification according to the law of Moses, they brought him up to Jerusalem to present him to the Lord. . . . Now there was a man in Jerusalem, whose name was Simeon, and this man was righteous and devout, looking for the consolation of Israel, and the Holy Spirit was upon him. . . . And inspired by the Spirit he came into the temple; and when the parents brought in the child Jesus, to do for him according to the custom of the law, he took him up in his arms and blessed God (*Luke 2:22, 25, 27, 28*).

Meditation

Mary and Joseph felt highly honored and favored of God, when the baby Jesus came into their home. It was a sober, sacred privilege which they shared with God. As parents they would have to provide the right kind of family life, education, counsel, and spiritual climate in order to prepare Jesus for His God-given work. Therefore, when they brought the baby Jesus to the temple for the blessing of Simeon, they also dedicated themselves to the sacred responsibility.

Dear parents, the privilege of parenthood is God-given and you will be responsible to Him for the way you rear your child. Fitting it is, therefore, that you have come to present this child for the blessing of God, and to dedicate yourselves as Christian parents before Him.

Responsive Litany

Minister and Congregation: (in unison) As a household of faith in the family of God, we members of this church congratulate you who bring these children of your love and the love of the Heavenly Father. We wish each of you to feel in your heart that you are doing a very important thing in thus presenting your children to the Lord in His sanctuary, even as the child Jesus was presented in the temple. Be assured that God is pleased with this beautiful observance of the ancient custom. And know in your heart that God will hear every prayer for these children who are dedicated unto Him on this day.

Minister: Do you members of this church receive these children in the name of the Lord, Jesus Christ, and promise to be unto them father, mother, brother, sister, friend?

Congregation: In the name of the Lord, Jesus Christ, we do.

Minister: And now, do you parents dedicate this child unto the Lord God; and do you promise as an elder child of the Heavenly Father to pray for and with your child, that he or she may grow in the knowledge and love of God?

Parents: I do.

Minister: Do you rededicate your home as a sacred

shrine and with a Christian environment in which the spiritual nature of your child may grow and unfold; and promise to do all you can by precept and example to lead your child at the proper age to a public confession of the Lord Jesus Christ, and to obedience to His Will?

Parents: I do.

Dedication Prayer

Heavenly Father, in whose love our earthly parenthood takes on meaning: We thank Thee for the gift of children. We would place these before Thee, most Holy God. Thou dost yearn for their fellowship, that they should know Thee, and serve Thy Kingdom.

Grant to these parents, we beseech Thee, wisdom, patience, justice, truth, and faith in guiding these lives physically, mentally, and spiritually to give glory to Thy Son, our Saviour, Jesus Christ. Amen.

Presentation of Children

(Children may then be given to the minister one by one for blessing.)

Minister: The name of this child is _____. The parents are _____.

Now may the blessings of Almighty God be upon you, both now and in the life everlasting. Amen.

Dedication Solo

"This Child We Dedicate to Thee"
(*tune—Federal Street*)

This child we dedicate to Thee
O God of grace and purity.
In Thy great love its life prolong,
Shield it, we pray, from sin and wrong.

O may Thy Spirit gently draw
Its willing soul to keep Thy law;
May virtue, piety, and truth
Dawn even with its dawning youth.

We, too, in Thy most gracious sight
Once shared this blessed holy rite
And would renew its solemn vow
We give Thee thanks, and praises now.

Grant that with true and faithful heart,
We may still act the Christian's part,
Follow the path the Master trod,
And ever do Thy will, O God. Amen.[1]

BRIEF DEDICATION SERVICE FOR INFANT AND PARENTS WITH SPONSORS

Mr. and Mrs. _____, you have brought (*child's name*) into the house of God today for this appointed moment, and thus you declare it to be your purpose to dedicate both yourselves and the child to the Christian way of life.

The Scriptures command that parents should bring up their children in the "nurture and admonition of the Lord." As a church we commend you for this high ideal and worthy purpose.

May God grant to both of you the wisdom and patience, the love and strength to accomplish this noble dream for your little one.

Mr. and Mrs. (*name of sponsors*), it is conceivable that these parents, in spite of their own very best intentions and efforts, may need help and guidance in their high endeavor; or that in the event of misfortune to one or both of them, (*child's name*) may need additional guardianship. By your presence here at this appointed time and place, you thus indicate your willingness to accept this responsibility; and if the need arises, to help train this child in the nurture and admonition of the Lord.

We often read in the Scriptures of the aid given within the family groups or friendship circles. May God also grant to you the fulfillment of your ideals and dreams for (*child's name*).

When Jesus was here in person among men on earth, as a babe He was presented in the temple. The prophet Simeon took the baby Jesus in his arms and prayed thankfully to God. When Jesus was grown to manhood, there are two things He did. He took the children in His arms and blessed them. Then He taught the older folk saying, "Unless you turn and become like children, you will never enter the kingdom of heaven. Whoever humbles himself like this child, he is greatest in the kingdom of heaven. Whoever receives one such child in my name, receives me. . . ." What grown-up would not give much if he could only restore to himself the innocence, trust, and faith of childhood.

Jesus is not here today in flesh, so He cannot take this baby in His arms, nor bless it by His voice. Neither is there present one of the prophets of old. However, a minister of the Master's church is here, and will take the little one in his arms (*minister takes the babe*). He will ask the Saviour's blessing on both babe and parent as we pray.

We humbly beseech Thee, Lord our God, that Thy Spirit may be upon this child, and dwell in *him* forever. Take *him* under Thy fatherly care, and grant *him* to grow in wisdom as in stature, and in favor with God and man. Give unto Thy servants to whom Thou hast committed this trust, the assurance of Thine unfailing grace. Guide them with Thy counsel as they teach and train their child to honor Thee, most Holy God. Amen.[2]

CHRISTMAS DEDICATION FOR INFANT
AND PARENTS

Scripture

And the angel said to her, "Do not be afraid, Mary, for you have found favor with God. And behold, you will conceive in your womb and bear a son, and you shall call his name Jesus. He will be great, and will be called the Son of the Most High; and the Lord God will give to him the throne of his father David, and he will reign over the house of Jacob for ever; and of his kingdom there will be no end. . . . But Mary kept all these things, pondering them in her heart (*Luke 1:30-33; 2:19*).

Meditation

There is nothing more heavenly than planning for a child, dreaming about a child, or becoming the parent of a child. Before a child, the big feel small and the proud, insignificant. A mother's deepest thoughts are never completely disclosed and a father's pride is never completely concealed, when a baby is born to them.

Kahlil Gibran has the "Prophet" speak to you about children. He says, "Your children are not your children, they are the sons and daughters of Life's longing for itself. They came through you but not from you. And though they are with you yet they belong not to you. You may give them your love but not your thoughts, for they have their own thoughts. You may house their bodies but not their souls, for their souls dwell in the house of tomorrow, which you cannot visit, not even in your dreams. You may strive to be like them, but seek not to make them like you. For life goes not backward nor tarries with yesterday. You are the bows from which your children as living arrows are sent forth. The archer sees the mark upon the path of the infinite and He bends you with His might that His arrows may go swift and far. Let your bending in the Archer's hand be for gladness; for even as He loves the arrow that flies, so He loves also the bow that is stable."[8]

Parents' Dedication

Do you, Mr. and Mrs. _____, promise that you will train this child in body, mind, and soul for service and fellowship with God?

Response: I do.

Do you promise to teach this child the principles of our Christian religion, and that you will pray with *him* and for *him?*

Response: I do.

Dedication Prayer

Our Father in Heaven, in whose image we have been made: We thank Thee for the gift of this young life who has blessed these parents. Though we do not understand the mystery of physical birth, our Father, we confess we have experienced a bit of heaven in this one's arrival. Though we do not understand completely the human mind and soul, yet we do recognize before Thee our responsibility in providing for this one given to our care.

Grant to these parents, we pray, the patience, good judgment, character, and discipline needed in guiding this life as Thou would have. Bless the child with a strong body, sound mind, and sensitive spirit. May the example and prayers of Christian friends ever be an encouragement and support.

With all the joy and solemnity of this moment, we

would now place the child before Thee, most Holy God, to be as Thou would have, in Jesus' name. Amen.

Blessing of Child

   (*Minister may take babe in his arms*)
   What is the name of this child?
   (*Child's name*), may the grace of the Lord Jesus Christ, and the love of God the Father, and the communion and fellowship of the Holy Spirit, be with you throughout your life. O Lord, grant unto these parents the grace to perform that which they have promised before Thee. Amen.

Lord's Prayer (in unison)

   Our Father which art in heaven, Hallowed be thy name. Thy kingdom come. Thy will be done on earth, as it is in heaven. Give us this day our daily bread. And forgive us our debts, as we forgive our debtors. And lead us not into temptation, but deliver us from evil: For thine is the kingdom, and the power, and the glory, for ever. Amen.

VIII. The Funeral

THE INITIAL CALL FOLLOWING DEATH

   Remember the promise of Scripture, "We know that in everything God works for good with those who love him" (*Romans 8:28a*).

   Prayer at the Home: Heavenly Father, from whom we

have come and unto whom we all must return: Thou alone dost understand the sense of loss which has been sustained by these dear people. Into Thy care we commit them. We would not have Thee remove their grief, but wilt Thou bind up their broken hearts with faith, and an awareness of Thy presence. Sustain them in these hours, and may their loss not seem more real than the gain that has come to their beloved, we pray in the name of Him who said, "Because I live, you, too, shall live." Amen.

OPENING SENTENCES FOR PUBLIC SERVICE

The eternal God is your dwelling place, and underneath are the everlasting arms (*Deuteronomy 33:27*).

Jesus said to her, "I am the resurrection and the life; he who believes in me, though he die, yet shall he live, and whoever lives and believes in me shall never die" (*John 11:25, 26*).

Our help is in the name of the Lord, who made heaven and earth (*Psalm 124:8*). And now has manifested through the appearing of our Savior Christ Jesus, who abolished death and brought life and immortality to light through the gospel (*II Timothy 1:10*).

The Lord is my light and my salvation; whom shall I fear? The Lord is the stronghold of my life; of whom shall I be afraid? (*Psalm 27:1*).

The Lord is near to all who call upon him, to all who call upon him in truth (*Psalm 145:18*).

Trust in the Lord for ever, for the Lord God is an everlasting rock (*Isaiah 26:4*).

The Benediction

The grace of our Lord Jesus Christ, and the love of God, and the communion of the Holy Spirit, be with you all. Amen.

ORDER FOR BAPTISM OF CHILDREN AND YOUTH

The Baptism Meditation

(*See selections*)

The Baptism Prayer

Almighty God, our Heavenly Father, who didst command the simple faith of the young: We present unto Thee this youth, who believing in Jesus Christ, now accepts Him as Lord and Saviour. Look with favor upon this dedication. Clothe *him,* we pray, with Thy whole armor—the breastplate of righteousness, the shield of faith, the helmet of salvation, and the sword of the spirit—that *he* may be able to withstand in the evil days, and having done all to stand. May Thy light preserve *him* from all error, and Thy power maintain *him* in perseverance. Make *his* life fruitful with good works so that *his* name may be written in the Lamb's Book of Life, to the glory of Jesus Christ the Lord. Amen.

Baptismal Pronouncement

By the authority of our Lord Jesus Christ, in whom you have confessed your faith, I baptize you, _____, in the name of the Father, and of the Son, and of the Holy Spirit. Amen.

The Baptism Blessing (to candidate)

The Lord bless you and keep you: The Lord make his face to shine upon you, and be gracious to you: The Lord lift up his countenance upon you, and give you peace (*Numbers 6:24-26*).

The Closing Sentence of Assurance (to witnesses)

There is therefore now no condemnation for those who are in Christ Jesus (*Romans 8:1*). Do you not know that all of us who have been baptized into Christ Jesus were baptized into his death? (*Romans 6:3*).

The Benediction

Now to him who is able to keep you from falling and to present you without blemish before the presence of his glory with rejoicing, to the only God, our Savior through Jesus Christ our Lord, be glory, majesty, dominion, and authority, before all time and now and for ever. Amen (*Jude 1:24, 25*).

ORDER FOR BAPTISM FOR INFANTS

Baptism Meditation

Hear the words of the gospel, written by Mark: And they were bringing children to him, that he might touch them; and the disciples rebuked them. But when Jesus saw it he was indignant, and said to them, "Let the children come to me, do not hinder them; for to such belongs the kingdom of God. Truly, I say to you, whoever does not receive the kingdom of God like a child shall not enter it." And he took them in his arms and blessed them, laying his hands upon them.

(*To parents*): Forasmuch as this child is now presented by you for baptism, and is thus consecrated to God and to His church, it is your part and duty to see that *he* be taught the meaning and purpose of this holy sacrament; that *he* be instructed in the principles of our holy faith and the nature of the Christian life, that *he* shall be trained to give reverent attendance upon the public and private worship of God and the teachings of the Holy Scripture, and that in every way, by precept and example, you shall seek to lead *him* in the love of God and the service of our Lord Jesus Christ.

Do you solemnly promise to fulfill these duties so far as in you lies, the Lord being your helper?

Response: We do.

The Baptismal Pronouncement

(*The minister takes child in arms*)

—————, I baptize thee in the name of the Father, and of the Son, and of the Holy Spirit. Amen.

The Closing Words of Assurance (to witnesses)

You, the people of this congregation, in receiving this child promise with God's help to be *his* sponsor to the end that *he* may confess Christ as *his* Lord and come at last to His eternal Kingdom.

The Baptismal Prayer

Heavenly Father, who hast promised that Thou wilt not only be our God, but also the God and Father of our children: Unto Thee we present this child. Take *him,* we entreat Thee, under Thy Fatherly care. Abundantly enrich *him* with Thy heavenly grace, bring *him* safely through the perils of childhood, deliver *him* from the temptations of youth, lead *him* to witness a good confession, to grow in wisdom as in stature, in favor with God and man, and to persevere therein to the end. Uphold the parents with loving care, wise counsel, and holy example through Jesus Christ.

The Benediction

Now to him who by the power at work within us is able to do far more abundantly than all that we ask or think, to him be glory in the church and in Christ Jesus to all generations, for ever and ever. Amen (*Ephesians 3:20, 21*).[1]

BAPTISM MEDITATIONS AND PRAYERS

A Sign of Obedience

Scripture: Jesus came and said to them, "All authority in heaven and on earth has been given to me. Go therefore and make disciples of all nations, baptizing them in the name of the Father and of the Son and of the Holy Spirit, teaching them to observe all that I have commanded you; and lo, I am with you always, to the close of the age (*Matthew 28:18, 19*).

Meditation: Baptism is a sign of humility and obedience to Jesus Christ. Apparently the Master thought it was extremely important. He Himself, though sinless, walked over sixty miles round trip to be baptized, as He said, "to fulfill all righteousness." He must have weighed carefully His closing words to the disciples which included the commission "to baptize."

Hence, in obedience to our Lord Jesus Christ, we now enter into this sacred act. Let us pray.

Prayer: Heavenly Father, whose will we have come to

know through Jesus Christ: We present to Thee the obedience of this Thy child, symbolized in this holy act. May it be more than obedience to outward form, but an allegiance to Thy Spirit, teachings and commands. May it be more than of the hour and day, but a faithfulness until death. Strengthen *him* in times of temptations, comfort *him* in sorrow, let Thy light shine upon *his* path. Through this surrender, O Lord, open a new dawn of opportunity and growth until *he* shall attain to the measure of the stature of the fulness of Jesus Christ, in whose name we pray. Amen.

Identified with Christ

Scripture: Do you not know that all of us who have been baptized into Christ Jesus were baptized into his death? We were buried therefore with him by baptism into death, so that as Christ was raised from the dead by the glory of the Father, we too might walk in newness of life (*Romans 6:3, 4*).

Meditation: One eminent Christian scholar has said, "Baptism is the embodiment of the gospel in one solemn act." It is a personal drama re-enacting the great saving acts of God in the death, burial, and resurrection of our Lord. It is the visible act by which you become identified with Christ. It is the outward expression of inward faith, by which you become dead as it were to sin, and are elevated to begin the supernatural life in fellowship with Christ. You will be united with Him, and nothing need separate you, not even death itself.

Prayer: Our God and Heavenly Father, we thank Thee for deliverance in Jesus Christ; for Thy love which gave Him in our behalf; for the power which raised Him victorious from the chains of the earth, and for this one who now in faith re-enacts Thy saving grace and unites *himself* with Thee. Grant that those who witness may discern the truth and hope of the gospel. By Thy mercy, we beseech Thee, grant this Thy child an inheritance imperishable, undefiled, and unfading, kept in heaven for all who love Thee, through Jesus Christ. Amen.

God's Wedding Ring

Scripture: In Christ Jesus you are all sons of God, through faith. For as many of you as were baptized into Christ have put on Christ. There is neither Jew nor Greek, there is neither slave nor free, there is neither male nor female; for you are all one in Christ Jesus (*Galatians 3:26-28*).

Meditation: There are three ways to become a part of a family. You can be born, adopted, or married into one. Baptism is the marriage ceremony by which we become a part of God's family.

A bride retains her maiden name until in a sacred ritual she pledges allegiance to a life companion and vows are exchanged. There is a uniting of minds and hearts, purposes and destinies. Then she takes the groom's name and becomes a member of his family.

Baptism, in a sense, is God's wedding ring. In this simple ceremony you are declaring your allegiance to Jesus Christ and uniting yourself to His purposes. You will wear His glorious name, and be a part of His earthly family.

Prayer: O Thou, by whom the whole family of heaven and earth is named: Accept into Thy fold this one who now pledges *her* fidelity, love, and devotion to Thee. Breathe upon *her* Thy Holy Spirit that *she* may never dishonor Thy family name. Seal Thy vows upon *her* heart. Sustain *her* in Thy grace by discipline. And may *her* love for Thee deepen in understanding, and *her* understanding into committed service, and *her* service into life eternal to the glory of Jesus Christ. Amen.

Commencing New Life

Scripture: Therefore, if any one is in Christ, he is a new creation; the old has passed away, behold, the new has come (*II Corinthians 5:17*).

Meditation: When Jesus Christ truly comes into a person's life, a complete revolution takes place in one's values, conduct, relationship with God, fellow men, and himself. So much so, that the old person is not even recognizable, hence is dead. The New Testament describes the Christian life as "putting off darkness, putting on light, putting off the old man with his deeds, and putting on the new man."

Baptism, which symbolizes the burial of the old life with its habits and the beginning of a new life in Christ, will leave an indelible psychological impression upon your mind so that you will not easily forget the meaning of Christian commitment.

Prayer: Gracious and merciful Father: We present unto Thee this Thy child, who believing upon Jesus Christ Thy Son, repenting of all sin and desiring to obey all Thy commands, would walk in newness of life. Forgive *his* past, O Lord. Grant that all sinful affections may die, and that belonging to Thee, *he* may add to *his* faith virtue, and to virtue knowledge, and to knowledge temperance, and to temperance patience, and to patience godliness and to godliness brotherly kindness, and to brotherly kindness, charity. Thus, may *he* experience the new life and live abundantly in the everlasting Kingdom of our Lord and Saviour, Jesus Christ. Amen.

Inward Cleansing

Scripture: Repent, and be baptized every one of you in the name of Jesus Christ for the forgiveness of your sins; and you shall receive the gift of the Holy Spirit (*Acts 2:38*).

Meditation: To portray the deeper spiritual meaning of God's forgiveness, water is used in baptism. Baptism is a symbol, not for the bathing of the body, but for cleansing the inward life. It is moral cleansing. In Christ, one finds pardon for the sins of the past; they are separated from Him as far as east is from west. In baptism you symbolize the cleansing of your mind, the purifying of your motives and the washing of your sins away by the power of Jesus Christ, in order that you may develop a new spirit, new purposes, and a new life.

Prayer: Gracious and merciful heavenly Father: We present unto Thee this one, who believing in Jesus Christ Thy Son as Saviour and repenting of and renouncing all sin, would obey Him in all that He commands. As *he* now surrenders *himself* unto Christ, cleanse *him* of *his* past, forgive *him his* sins, and fill *him* with Thy Holy Spirit of light and power. Preserve *him* from all error that *he* may be maintained in the patience, perseverance, and victory of Thy saints, and may *he* have a place with those of every nation who, coming out of great tribulation, have washed their robes and made them white in the blood of the Lamb. Amen.

VI. Marriage

A FORM FOR SOLEMNIZATION OF MARRIAGE

When the persons to be married have come before the minister, he shall say:

We are met in the presence of God to unite this man and this woman by the sacred ties of matrimony. Let us pray:

God, be merciful unto us and bless us, and cause His face to shine upon us, through Jesus Christ our Lord. Amen.

Becoming more sacred in the estimation of men, marriage has existed from the beginning of human history. It has the sanction of heaven, having been instituted by God and honored by Jesus of Nazareth, and it should have the approbation of all. From it, "founded in reason, loyal, just and pure, have sprung all the sweet charities of family and home, and the uplifting and refining influences that flow out from them."

Those who take its vows are brought into the closest and most sacred of human relationships. Their lives are blended into one as the waters of confluent streams are mingled, and thenceforth, they must share the joys and sorrows of life. And from this close and intimate relationship spring obligations of the most solemn and lasting character. The husband is under obligations to throw around the wife his protecting care, to shield her from the rough storms of the world, to cling to her with unfaltering fidelity, to cherish her with unfailing affection, and to guard her happiness with unceasing vigilance. And the wife is under obligation to love and cherish her husband, to honor and sustain him, and to be true to him in all ways. Each is under obligation to fulfill the love ordained of God as recorded in I Corinthians 13.

"This love of which I speak is slow to lose patience—it looks for a way of being constructive. It is not possessive: it is neither anxious to impress nor does it cherish inflated ideas of its own importance. Love has good manners and does not pursue selfish advantage. It is not touchy. It does not compile statistics of evil or gloat over the wickedness of other people. On the contrary, it is glad with all good men when Truth prevails. Love knows no limit to its endurance, no end to its trust, no fading of its hope; it can outlast anything. It is, in fact, the one thing that still stands when all else has fallen" (I Corinthians 13:4-7, PHILLIPS).

Then the Minister shall say: Who giveth this woman to be the bride of this man?

Then the father, or whoever takes his place, shall answer: I do. (Or, Her mother and I do.)

And now, if you, knowing of nothing either legal or moral to forbid your union in marriage, wish to take its vows and assume its obligations, indicate that wish by joining your right hands.

Their hands being clasped, the minister shall ask the man:

Will you, _____, have this woman _____, whose hand you hold to be your wedded wife, and solemnly promise that you will loyally fulfill your obligations as her husband to protect her, honor her, love her, and cherish her in adversity as well as in prosperity and keep yourself unto her alone, so long as you both shall live?

The man shall answer: I will.

Then the minister shall ask the woman: Will you,
————————, have this man ———————— whose hand you hold
to be your wedded husband and solemnly promise that
you will be unto him a tender, loving, and true wife
through sunshine and shadow alike, and be faithful to him
so long as you both shall live?

The woman shall answer: I will.

Let us pray: Almighty God, heavenly Father of mankind, whose nature is love: Look with favor upon this man
and this woman who desire now to make their vows before
Thee. We are grateful for the families that have reared
them to maturity, the church which has nurtured them
with ideals, and the Providence which has led them to this
happy and holy altar of marriage. Grant this to be more
than an outward union, but rather the blending of hearts
and spirits and purposes. Bless each with the inward qual-
ities of loyalty, honor, purity, self-control, trust, cooperation, and forgiveness, that they may keep faithfully this
holy covenant, and may live together all their days in true
love and perfect peace, through Jesus Christ the Master of
the art of living, and our Saviour. Amen.

*Then shall they loose their hands and move to the altar,
and the minister shall say:* We read in the old story that
when God made a covenant with Noah, He set a bow in
the cloud as a token thereof, and said, "I will look upon it,
that I may remember the everlasting covenant." From this
we may learn that it is well for us, when we enter into
solemn agreement one with another, to set apart some reminder of what we have promised. As tokens of your
marriage covenant, you have each selected a ring of gold.

*Here the ring (or rings) shall be given to the minister
and he shall say:* Gold, precious among metals, fittingly

represents the precious ties that unite husband and wife. These (this) rings (ring), endless until broken by outside forces, are (is a) fit symbols (symbol) of the unbroken partnership of marriage which should continue until broken by death. Let them (it) be unto you constant reminders (a constant reminder) of your obligations to each other, and mute incentives (a mute incentive) to their fulfillment.

Then the minister shall say to the man: Forasmuch as the husband imparts to his wife his name and receives her into his care and keeping, I give you this ring. Put it upon the wedding finger of your bride, and say to her these words: I, _____, give this ring to you, _____, and by this act declare, in the presence of these witnesses, that I take you to be my beloved wife; that I will be unto you a faithful husband until death shall part us.

Then the minister shall say to the woman: Take the ring which you have selected, put it upon the wedding finger of your bridegroom, and say to him these words: I, _____, give this ring to you, _____, (if single ring ceremony, the woman will say: I, _____, receive this ring from you, _____,) and thus declare, in the presence of these witnesses that you are the husband of my choice, that I will be faithful to you until death shall part us.

Thus, you are to wear these rings (this ring) as the enclosing bond of reverence and trust. You both are to fulfill the perfect circle of duty that makes you one. As you hope for happiness in your married life, I charge you to be true to the vows you have taken. With your marriage, you begin life under new conditions and with larger responsibilities; and it is only by faithfully performing the duties and fulfilling the obligations of the new relation that true and lasting happiness can be found.

Forasmuch as you, _____, and you, _____, have openly declared your wishes to be united in marriage, and in the presence of God, and before these witnesses have pledged love and fidelity each to the other, and have confirmed the same by each giving and receiving a ring, and by joining hands, I, as a minister of Christ's Church and legally authorized so to do by the State of _____, pronounce now that you are Husband and Wife.

To the man: Guard well this woman who now commits herself to your keeping, and strive so to live that no word or deed of yours shall cloud her brow with sorrow or dim her eyes with tears or grief. *To the woman:* And you strive to retain by your virtures the heart you have won by your graces. *To both:* Let not your voices lose the tender tones of affection. Let not "your eyes forget the gentle ray they wore in courtship's smiling day." So you will find in your union an unfailing source of joy, being one in name, one in aim, and one in happy destiny together.

Let us kneel: Entreat me not to leave you or to return from following you; for where you go I will go, and where you lodge I will lodge; your people shall be my people, and your God my God (*Ruth 1:16*).

The Lord bless you and keep you; the Lord make His face to shine upon you, and be gracious unto you; the Lord lift up His countenance upon you and give you peace. Amen.[1]

A FORM FOR SOLEMNIZATION OF MATRIMONY ACCORDING TO THE BOOK OF COMMON PRAYER

At the day and time appointed for solemnization of Matrimony, the Persons to be married shall come into the body of the Church, or shall be ready in some proper house, with their friends and neighbors; and there standing together, the Man on the right hand, and the Woman on the left, the Minister shall say,

Dearly beloved, we are gathered together here in the sight of God, and in the face of this company, to join together this Man and this Woman in holy Matrimony; which is an honourable estate, instituted of God, signifying unto us the mystical union that is betwixt Christ and his Church: which holy estate Christ adorned and beautified with his presence and first miracle that he wrought in Cana of Galilee, and is commended of Saint Paul to be honourable among all men: and therefore is not by any to be entered into unadvisedly or lightly; but reverently, discreetly, advisedly, soberly, and in the fear of God. Into this holy estate these two persons present come now to be joined. If any man can show just cause, why they may not lawfully be joined together, let him now speak, or else hereafter for ever hold his peace.

And also speaking unto the Persons who are to be married, he shall say,

I require and charge you both, as ye will answer at the dreadful day of judgment when the secrets of all hearts shall be disclosed, that if either of you know any impediment, why ye may not be lawfully joined together in Matrimony, ye do now confess it. For be ye well assured, that if any persons are joined together otherwise than as God's Word doth allow, their marriage is not lawful.

The Minister, if he shall have reason to doubt of the lawfulness of the proposed Marriage, may demand sufficient surety for his indemnification: but if no impediment shall be alleged, or suspected, the Minister shall say to the Man,

——————, wilt thou have this Woman to be thy wedded wife, to live together after God's ordinance in the holy estate of Matrimony? Wilt thou love her, comfort her,

our Lord to His church. So then you are no longer a stranger and sojourner, but you are a fellow citizen with the saints and members of the household of God.

Now that you have publicly signified your desire to fellowship with this congregation in its worship and work, on behalf of this church, I receive and welcome you, —————, in the name of our Lord Jesus Christ, and present to you the right hand of fellowship. Be strong in the Lord and in the strength of His might.

PERSON RENEWING HIS CHRISTIAN COVENANT

If we confess our sins, he is faithful and just, and will forgive our sins and cleanse us from all unrighteousness (*I John 1:9*).

Having truly repented of your sins, —————, do you reaffirm your confession of Jesus as the Christ, the Son of the living God, and do you now renew your covenant of faithfulness and service to Him as your Lord and Saviour?

Response: I do.

If we walk in the light, as he is in the light, we have fellowship with one another, and the blood of Jesus his Son cleanses us from all sin (*I John 1:7*).

A MEMBERSHIP (OR CONFIRMATION) CLASS

We are now to receive these who have had instruction in the teachings of the church, and now of their own accord desire to take upon themselves the vows and privileges of discipleship.

Before you are admitted into the church, it becomes my duty to inquire of you as to your purposes of mind and heart.

Do you believe in God as your Heavenly Father?

Response: I do.

Do you accept Jesus as your Saviour and Lord?
Response: I do.

Will you strive to know and to do the will of God as taught in the Holy Scriptures?
Response: I will.

Will you be loyal to the church, wherever you are, and uphold it by your prayers, your presence, your gifts and your services?

Response: I will.

I extend to you the right hand of fellowship and welcome you into the fellowship of this congregation.

May God bless you for this commitment to Him who is above every name.

BAPTISM ORDER

ORDER FOR BAPTISM OF ADULTS

The Baptism Meditation and Prayer

(*See selections*)

The Baptism Pronouncement

—————, upon your confession of faith in the Lord Jesus Christ and in obedience to His divine command, I baptize you in the name of the Father, Son, and Holy Spirit. Amen.

The Baptismal Blessing (to candidate)

May the joy of Jesus Christ our Lord make full your joy. Let your heart rejoice in the salvation of God.

The Closing Sentence of Assurance (to witnesses)

[Jesus] became the source of eternal salvation to all who obey him (*Hebrews 5:9b*). Therefore, be imitators of God, as beloved children (*Ephesians 5:1*).

He who dwells in the shelter of the Most High, who abides in the shadow of the Almighty, will say to the Lord, "My refuge and my fortress; my God, in whom I trust" (*Psalm 91:1-2*).

God is our refuge and strength, a very present help in trouble. Therefore we will not fear (*Psalm 46:1, 2a*).

INVOCATIONS

Ever living God, before whose face pass the generations of men, whose mercies are from everlasting to everlasting: Thou hast taught that in quietness and confidence shall be our strength; by the power of Thy Spirit, lift us to Thy presence, where we may be still and know that Thou art God, through Jesus Christ the Lord. Amen.

Eternal Spirit, in whom we live and move and have our being, in whom our life is Thy joy, and death only an incident in the eternal adventure to which Thou callest us: Bring light out of the darkness, hope out of our sorrow, and comfort that rises out of an awareness of Thy presence, we pray in the Spirit of Jesus. Amen.[1]

Thou who art the God of the living; to whom there are no dead; in whose sight those whom we call dead are still alive: We offer thanks to Thee who giveth us the victory, through Him who lives though He was dead; even Jesus Christ our Lord. Amen.

Our Father in heaven, Thou art the refuge of the distressed, and the helper of the needy: Out of the depth of our present grief we turn to Thee, praying that the light of Thy countenance will shine upon us, a sense of Thy presence will strengthen us, and the reality of the unseen world will console us, through Jesus Christ, who conquered death, we pray. Amen.

Almighty and Eternal God, who amid the changes of this mortal life art always the same: We bow in reverence before Thee. In the silence of this hour, speak to us of eternal things and comfort us with the assurance of Thine everlasting love, through Jesus Christ our Lord. Amen.

SCRIPTURE READINGS

Glorious Assurance

The Lord is my shepherd, I shall not want. . . . Even though I walk through the valley of the shadow of death, I fear no evil, for thou art with me; thy rod and thy staff they comfort me (*Psalm 23:1, 4*). For this perishable nature must put on the imperishable, and this mortal nature must put on immortality. When the perishable puts on the imperishable, and the mortal puts on immortality, then shall come to pass the saying that is written: "Death is swallowed up in victory" (*I Corinthians 15:53, 54*). Neither death, nor life, nor angels, nor principalities, nor things present, nor things to come, nor powers, nor height, nor depth, nor anything else in all creation, will be able to separate us from the love of God in Christ Jesus our Lord (*Romans 8:38, 39*). Let not your hearts be troubled; believe in God, believe also in me. In my Father's house are many rooms; if it were not so, would I have told you that I go to prepare a place for you? And when I go and prepare a place for you, I will come again and will take you to myself, that where I am you may be also (*John 14:1-3*). And death shall be no more, neither shall there be mourning and crying nor pain any more, for the former things have passed away. . . . They shall hunger no more, neither thirst any more; the sun shall not strike them nor any scorching heat. For the Lamb in the midst of the throne will be their shepherd, and he will guide them to springs of living water; and God will wipe away every tear from their eyes (*Revelation 21:4; 7:16, 17*).

Victory Over Tribulations

God is our refuge and strength, a very present help in trouble (*Psalm 46:1*). When you pass through the waters I will be with you; and through the rivers, they shall not overwhelm you; when you walk through fire you shall not be burned, and the flame shall not consume you. For I am the Lord your God (*Isaiah 43:2, 3a*). He said, "The Lord is my rock, and my fortress, and my deliverer, my God, my rock, in whom I take refuge, my shield and the horn of my salvation, my stronghold and my refuge, my savior (*II Samuel 22:2, 3*). What then shall we say to this? If God is for us, who is against us? He who did not spare his own Son but gave him up for us all, will he not also give us all things with him? Who shall bring any charge against God's elect? It is God who justifies; who is to condemn? Is it Christ Jesus, who died, yes, who was raised from the dead, who is at the right hand of God, who indeed intercedes for us? Who shall separate us from the love of Christ? Shall tribulation, or distress, or persecution, or famine, or nakedness, or peril, or sword? . . . No, in all these things we are more than conquerors through him who loved us (*Romans 8:31-35, 37*). For this slight momentary affliction is preparing for us an eternal weight of glory beyond all comparison, because we look not to the things that are seen but to the things that are unseen; for the things that are seen are transient, but the things that are unseen are eternal (*II Corinthians 4:17-18*).

The Resurrected Life

But we would not have you ignorant, brethren, concerning those who are asleep, that you may not grieve as others do who have no hope. For since we believe that Jesus died and rose again, even so, through Jesus, God will bring with him those who have fallen asleep (*I Thessalonians 4:13-14*). If in this life we who are in Christ have only hope, we are of all men most to be pitied. But in fact Christ has been raised from the dead, the first fruits of those who have fallen asleep (*I Corinthians 15:19, 20*). What is sown is perishable, what is raised is imperishable. It is sown in dishonor, it is raised in glory. It is sown in weakness, it is raised in power. It is sown a physical body, it is raised a spiritual body. If there is a physical body, there is also a spiritual body. Thus it is written, "The first man Adam became a living being"; the last Adam became a life-giving spirit (*I Corinthians 15:42-45*). Just as we have borne the image of the man of dust, we shall also bear the image of the man of heaven. I tell you this, brethren: flesh and blood cannot inherit the kingdom of God, nor does the perishable inherit the imperishable. Lo! I tell you a mystery. We shall not all sleep, but we shall all be changed, in a moment, in the twinkling of an eye, at the last trumpet. For the trumpet will sound, and the dead will be raised imperishable, and we shall be changed. For this perishable nature must put on the imperishable, and this mortal nature must put on immortality (*I Corinthians 15:49-53*). But thanks be to God who gives us the victory through our Lord Jesus Christ. Therefore, my beloved brethren, be steadfast, immovable, always abounding in the work of the Lord, knowing that in the Lord your labor is not in vain (*I Corinthians 15:57, 58*).

God's Provisions

The Lord is my light and my salvation; whom shall I fear? The Lord is the stronghold of my life; of whom shall I be afraid? (*Psalm 27:1*). When I am afraid, I put my trust in thee. In God, whose word I praise, in God I trust without a fear. What can flesh do to me? (*Psalm 56:3, 4*). I heard a voice from heaven saying, "Write this: Blessed are the dead who die in the Lord henceforth." "Blessed indeed," says the Spirit, "that they may rest from their labors, for their deeds follow them!" (*Revelation 14:13*). But, as it is written, "What no eye has seen, nor ear heard, nor the heart of man conceived, what God has prepared for those who love him" (*I Corinthians 2:9*). Then the King will say to those at his right hand, "Come, O blessed of my Father, inherit the kingdom prepared for you from the foundation of the world; for I was hungry and you gave me food, I was thirsty and you gave me drink, I was a stranger and you welcomed me, I was naked and you clothed me, I was sick and you visited me, I was in prison and you came to me. . . . Truly, I say to you, as you did it to one of the least of these my brethren, you did it to me" (*Matthew 25:34-36, 40*). Then I saw a new heaven and a new earth; for the first heaven and the first earth had passed away, and the sea was no more. And I saw the holy city, new Jerusalem, coming down out of heaven from God, prepared as a bride adorned for her husband; and I heard a great voice from the throne saying, "Behold, the dwelling of God is with men. He will dwell with them, and they shall be his people, and God himself will be with them (*Revelation 21:1-3*). For we know that if the earthly tent we live in is destroyed, we have a building from God, a house not made with hands, eternal in the heavens (*II Corinthians 5:1*).

True Security

Do not lay up for yourselves treasures on earth, where moth and rust consume and where thieves break in and steal, but lay up for yourselves treasures in heaven, where neither moth nor rust consumes and where thieves do not break in and steal. For where your treasure is, there will your heart be also (*Matthew 6:19-21*). A man's life does not consist in the abundance of his possessions (*Luke 12:15*). For what will it profit a man, if he gains the whole world and forfeits his life? (*Matthew 16:26*). Blessed are the poor in spirit, for theirs is the kingdom of heaven. Blessed are those who mourn, for they shall be comforted. Blessed are the meek, for they shall inherit the earth. Blessed are those who hunger and thirst for righteousness, for they shall be satisfied. Blessed are the merciful, for they shall obtain mercy. Blessed are the pure in heart, for they shall see God. Blessed are the peacemakers, for they shall be called sons of God. Blessed are those who are persecuted for righteousness' sake, for theirs is the kingdom of heaven. Blessed are you when men revile you and persecute you and utter all kinds of evil against you falsely on my account. Rejoice and be glad, for your reward is great in heaven, for so men persecuted the prophets who were before you (*Matthew 5:3-12*). Every one then who hears these words of mine and does them will be like a wise man who built his house upon the rock; and the rain fell, and the floods came, and the winds blew and beat upon that house, but it did not fall, because it had been founded on the rock. And every one who hears these words of mine and does not do them will be like a foolish man who built his house upon the sand; and the rain fell, and the floods came, and the winds blew and beat against that house, and it fell; and great was the fall of it (*Matthew 7:24-27*).

PASTORAL FUNERAL PRAYERS

Thou who art the author of our being, the One whose thought designed our existence, whose purpose has awakened in us a response to truth and a longing for perfection: We bow before Thee. Deep in us, O God, is a sense of our incompleteness. Within us we have experienced aspirations that can never be satisfied in this world. Grant that we may see in death the opportunity for completed purposes, fuller attainment, clearer insight, and perfection of imperfection. May we realize in Christ the life that death cannot take away, nor the grave destroy. Amen.

O Thou who canst turn the shadows of night into morning, and who art a refuge for Thy children in their affliction: Enable those upon whom this death so closely falls to know the love of Christ, to believe in the reality of the unseen, and to find inward strength to meet their affliction. Amen.

We thank Thee for the truth of Thy gospel and the great hope of eternal life confirmed by the resurrection of our Lord, Jesus Christ. For that inheritance where there is no pain, where parting is unknown, and death is no more, we would commit ourselves through our remaining days, until we see Thee, our Maker, face to face. Amen.

The Lord is my shepherd; I shall not want. In Thee we live and move and have our being; in Thee is our trust for all we need. Thou art our all in all; beyond Thee we have no need. *He maketh me to lie down in green pastures; He leadeth me beside the still waters.* From Thee we have received all that makes life rich and good. We thank Thee for precious moments of silence and reverence in which Thou dost speak, and for the comfort of good friends and for inward peace. *He restoreth my soul.* When the world is too much for us, or we are weary of welldoing and life is saddened with sorrows and pain and fear—Thou restoreth our spirit and dost lift us up. *He leadeth me in the paths of righteousness.* When the hurry of the day makes us thoughtless of others and when we think too much of that which is our own, Thou hast led us back to the paths of unselfishness and what is right. *Yea, though I walk through the valley of the shadow of death, I will fear no evil: for thou art with me.* When we become sick, when life draws to a close, when empty places are left in our homes, Thou dost uphold us. *Thou preparest a table before me . . . My cup runneth over.* No power is so great, no threat so stern that we can be separated from Thee. In the midst of life's defeats, Thou art there to comfort. *Surely goodness and mercy shall follow me all the days of my life.* Thou hast promised not to leave us comfortless. Thou hast been with us in the past; Thou art our constant companion for the future. *And I will dwell in the house of the Lord forever.*[2]

COMMITTAL SERVICE AT GRAVESIDE

Scripture Sentences

For I know whom I have believed and I am sure that he is able to guard until that Day what has been entrusted to me (*II Timothy 1:12*).

Unless a grain of wheat falls into the earth and dies, it remains alone; but if it dies, it bears much fruit (*John 12:24*).

Jesus said, "I am the resurrection and the life; he who believes in me . . . shall never die" (*John 11:25, 26*).

Committal Sentence

Cherishing memories that are forever sacred, sustained by a faith that is stronger than death, and comforted by the hope of a life that shall endless be, all that is mortal of our friend we therefore commit to its resting place, amidst these beautiful surroundings of nature, in the assurance that if the earthly tent of our tabernacle be dissolved, we have a building from God, a house not made with hands, eternal in the heavens.

Committal Prayer

Soul of the Universe, Creator of life, Father of mankind, and of our Lord Jesus Christ: We commit back to nature all that which is natural and to the grave only that which the grave can hold. To Thee we commend the soul, trusting in Thy love, wisdom, and power. Comfort Thou Thy servants whose hearts are full, and grant that they may so love and serve Thee in this life that, together with Thy loved ones, they too may obtain the fullness of Thy promises in the world to come, through Jesus Christ our Lord. Amen.

BENEDICTIONS

To the King of ages, immortal, invisible, the only God, be honor and glory for ever and ever. Amen (*I Timothy 1:17*).

May Almighty God, the Father, the Son, and the Holy Spirit, bless you and keep you, now and for ever more. Amen.

And the peace of God, which passes all understanding, will keep your hearts and your minds in Christ Jesus (*Philippians 4:7*).

The grace of our Lord Jesus Christ, the love of God, and the communion of the Holy Spirit be with us all to the end, and in the end. Amen.

O Lord, support us all the day long of our troublous life until the shadows lengthen and the evening comes, and the busy world is hushed, and the fever of life is over, and our day's work is done. Then in Thy mercy grant us a safe lodging and a holy rest, and peace at the last. Amen.[3]

The peace of God, which passes all understanding, will keep your hearts and your minds in Christ Jesus. . . . To our God and Father be glory for ever and ever. Amen (*Philippians 4:7, 20*).

IX. Hospital Visitation

MEDITATIONS

UPON ENTERING THE HOSPITAL

Meditation: Although you may be in a place of strange scenes, sounds, odors, and experiences, yet you are not among strange people. You are not alone. God is with you. These doctors and nurses here in the hospital are your friends. By their kindly ways and years of required training, they have been helping friends back to health and strength. For a few days this will be your home. Home is a place of love, friends, peace, and those who care.[1]

A nurse is always on duty. If you ring for her, she will answer as soon as she is able. The doctors and attendants will respect your privacy and you need feel no embarrassment. As your minister, I will come to see you from time to time. If you feel you need me at any time, please tell the nurse to call me. Most people who enter a hospital are soon well and strong again. With God's help you can face whatever the day may bring. Practice the presence of the Heavenly Father; it can take away all the strangeness and make this a place of confidence and trust.

Scripture: Cast all your anxieties on him, for he cares about you (*I Peter 5:7*).

Pastor's Prayer: Kind God, merciful Father: We pause in gratitude for this sanctuary of healing, and for every expression of love and unselfish concern. Grant that we may see behind those who wait upon us the presence of the Great Physician, who was compassionate, faithful, and kind. Use the wisdom of the doctors, the vigilant care of the nurses, the healing power of medicine, and the re-creating influence of Thy Spirit; to hasten the recovery of this patient's health, we pray through Jesus Christ, the Lord. Amen.

Meditation: If all the facilities for "making people well" were seen at a glance, the sight would be astounding. If all the hospitals, equipment, laboratories, doctors, nurses, employees, money, and years of specialized training could be paraded before you, you would see what the world is doing for your recovery. The knowledge and experience of the past are at the doctor's disposal—for you.

The laws of nature are laws of healing. Bones knit. Wounds heal. Surgery gets rid of unwelcome "intruders" and lets nature do its normal work. All this is for you—and all others who are ill.[2]

Scripture: The Lord is near to all who call upon him (*Psalm 145:18*).

For God so loved the world that he gave his only Son, that whoever believes in him should not perish but have eternal life (*John 3:16*).

Bless the Lord, O my soul, and forget not all his benefits, who forgives all your iniquity, who heals all your diseases . . . who crowns you with steadfast love and mercy, who satisfies you with good as long as you live (*Psalm 103:2-5*).

Pastor's Prayer: Heavenly Father: How marvelous is the gift of life! In these quiet moments, we lift up our thoughts in gratitude for the dedication of men and women who have uncovered increasingly the mysteries of disease and have applied the best scientific insight to prolong the life span. We thank Thee for the progress made, and that this Thy child has had the good fortune of these benefits. Out of gratitude for these unmerited blessings, we would fill our days in useful service to Thee, through Jesus Christ. Amen.

BEFORE AN OPERATION

Meditation: As your body is being prepared for the coming surgery, allow God, your Creator, to prepare your mind. Relax and be at ease. As you trust your doctor and his assistants, so also trust the Great Physician. "Put your trust in the Lord." Have confidence in Him. "Bless the Lord, O my Soul . . . who healeth all thy diseases."

Let the "peace of God which passeth all understanding" be in your heart and mind. Let God do His work. "In quietness and confidence shall be your strength." You are God's child. He wants to help you in every way that you are capable of receiving His help. "Commit thy ways unto the Lord." Let Him speak peace to your heart.[3]

Scripture: Fear not, for I am with you (*Isaiah 43:5*).

Pastor's Prayer: Our Father, who art never far away: We face this experience in trust, believing that Thy power and love are sufficient for our needs. Strengthen Thou this patient with inner peace. As the surgeon's hands are cleansed, so wash away any sins lurking in our subconscious minds. Bless the surgeon with skill to match the need. We commend to Thy safekeeping our life, both now and evermore. Amen.

BIRTH OF A BABY

Meditation: In I Samuel, we read the account of Samuel's birth. Hannah and her husband, Elkanah, had no children. You know the pain and disappointment of having no children when your arms ache to hold one you can call your own. Hannah and Elkanah prayed earnestly to God that she might give birth to a son, vowing that if the prayer were answered the infant should be dedicated for life to Jehovah. The petition was granted, and they carried out their vow. They named the child Samuel, meaning "God given."

In a very real sense this child is yours, and yet not yours. It belongs to you and yet does not belong to you. Parenthood is a God-given privilege; He originated life. The wisdom of the Almighty has placed this life into your care to mold and make, develop and shape, to prepare for life on earth and in eternity. You will be responsible to God for how you rear your child. May you have the faith and wisdom to match this great opportunity.

Scripture: Mary, the mother of Jesus, expressed her gratitude in these words: "My soul magnifies the Lord, and my spirit rejoices in God my Savior . . . for he who is mighty has done great things for me, and holy is his name" (*Luke 1:46, 47, 49*).

Pastor's Prayer: Though we do not understand the mystery of physical birth, our Heavenly Father, we confess we have experienced a bit of heaven in this one's arrival. We thank Thee for Thy providence that has brought these to share in Thy creation, for the wondrous design of body and soul, and for the privilege of parenthood. Grant the child a strong body, a sound mind, and a sensitive spirit. Impress upon these parents the responsibility to Thee for the child's welfare, and bless them with patience, character, and good judgment, that this one may bring honor to Thee in the name of Jesus. Amen.

ONE HANDICAPPED

Meditation: There are two ways to catch a dagger thrown at you. You can catch it by the blade so that it injures you, or by the handle so that it becomes an instrument of defense.

So there are two ways to respond to life's unexpected disappointments. If we become bitter, cynical, resentful, it is like catching a dagger by the blade. We are not helped, but injured. Or we can respond creatively, making the best of the situation and using it for good.

Before Jesus endured the cross, men went to crosses to die. After He experienced the cross, He so transformed it that men now go there to live. He took the circumstance, as evil as it was, and made it a blessing to mankind: indeed, the cross became the symbol of God's power for man's redemption.

God can help you make this hospital stay, and whatever physical handicap you might sustain, a blessing in disguise. This experience can give you time to catch up on your thinking, reading, listening. It can be the beginning of a new spiritual life. Sometimes we are stricken down in order that we might move up, and we are forced to go back in order that we might go forward.

Scripture: God works in all things to bring about good to them that love the Lord.[4]

Pastor's Prayer: O Thou, who on Calvary's cross didst share our weakness, help us to share also Thy strength. Help us to approach this experience creatively in order that we might learn the lessons suffering has to teach, and may we thus derive spiritual depth. Grant that this one may not become bitter, but rather sweet; not complaining, but rather more humble and understanding; not cold and indifferent, but rather sympathetic and kind. Help *him* to know the power of Thy Spirit which is working in *him* now to bring about good and open new doors of opportunity, through Jesus Christ, who suffered for the sins of the world. Amen.

ONE CONVALESCING

Meditation: During recuperation, time may hang heavily on your hands. The following suggestions may help you:

See to how many people you can give encouragement or a sincere word of appreciation; look about you and count the evidences of God's handiwork; read your New Testament, note especially in Luke, Jesus' concern for those who had physical ailments; write notes of appreciation to those who have been concerned over your illness; express appreciation to the nurses for their work and care; make a list of things you resolve to do for others when you are well and they are ill; write a set of "hospital devotions" which you think would meet a practical need for others; give more time to prayer and personal devotions, praying especially for others in the hospital.[5]

Scripture: Bless the Lord, O my soul: and all that is within me, bless his holy name. Bless the Lord, O my soul, and forget not all his benefits: Who forgiveth all thine iniquities; who healeth all thy diseases; Who redeemeth thy life from destruction; who crowneth thee with lovingkindness and tender mercies (*Psalm 103:1-4,* AV).

Pastor's Prayer: Eternal God, our unfailing Guide and Friend, Thou who hast proven beyond our comprehension that Thou art our Father: In the lonely hours we have felt Thee near—so near as to share with us. In our anxiety, weariness and pain, we have had Thy peace and care and love. Thanks be unto Thee that Thy grace and power did minister to us. Thou art indeed the Good Shepherd, the Great Physician. The lesser things have dropped from view; the grander, nobler things have compelled our attention. All life has taken on new meaning. And now as we wait on Thee, give us patience, and be Thou patient with us a little longer. Set Thy purpose before us in all clarity. Renew us in health, in strength, in faith, as with a trustful spirit we look unto Thee. May this period of waiting be an opportunity of dedication. May Thy blessings, Lord, rest upon our beloved ones, upon all who have been in attendance, upon all who share the hospitality of this Temple of Healing. Keep us this day, tomorrow, and evermore, within Thy gracious keeping. Thine is the Kingdom, and the Power, and the Glory. Amen.[6]

ON FORGIVENESS

Meditation: Katherine Lee Bates has caught a frequent mood in her poem:

> Why art thou cast down, O my soul?
> Why art thou disquieted within me?
> Feelest thou not the Father nigh,
> Him whose heart contains us all?
> Lives not God for thee on high,
> Loving while His judgments fall?
>
> > Look above!
> > God is love!
>
> Not the Christ in the manger,
> Not the Christ on the cross
> But the Christ in the soul
> Shall save the soul
> When all but love is lost.[7]

Scripture: If we confess our sins, he is faithful and just to forgive us our sins, and to cleanse us from all unrighteousness (*I John 1:9,* AV).

Come now, let us reason together, says the Lord: though your sins are like scarlet, they shall be as white as snow; though they are red like crimson, they shall become like wool (*Isaiah 1:18*).

Pastor's Prayer: Merciful God, loving Father: In this secluded chapel of our soul where we may commune and not be heard, we would make our confession to Thee of selfishness, worry, thoughtlessness, and weakness. O Lord, who art more willing to forgive than we are ready to confess or to ask: be merciful, and forgive us. Create in us a clean heart, O God, and renew a right spirit within us. We wait now for Thy quiet word, "Go in peace, thou art whole again." With this assurance we wait the opportunity to exercise our sincere endeavor, in honor of Jesus Christ the Lord. Amen.

WHEN MORALE IS LOW

Meditation: One characteristic of sickness is its demoralizing effect on a person's thinking. Sometimes a brave man becomes cowardly, a strong man weak, and a poised person demoralized. Our ability to carry on becomes undermined. We fall easy victims to fears, worries, impatience, and other factors which normally we would put aside.

When one is ill he also loses his perspective. Today's pain seems eternal. Life's processes appear to be broken. It is difficult to realize that ten days or two weeks of sickness are but a small part of a year. After it is all over we recover balance and perspective. While we are ill we often lose poise. We lack the capacity to fit an unfortunate experience into the pattern of life.

Do not become discouraged. If you are a child of God you have already learned that all things work together for good for those who love God. Take life's blows with chin up and shoulders back. Your sickness is but a small part of a busy life. If you want to, you can learn much from this experience.[8]

Scripture: When I am afraid, I put my trust in thee (*Psalm 56:3*). Cast your burden on the Lord, and he will sustain you (*Psalm 55:22*).

Pastor's Prayer: O Lord, it is so easy to become discouraged and defeated. In Thine own way, wilt Thou do for this one what *he* cannot do for *himself*. Give *him* the courage and patience to endure one minute at a time, then one hour, then one day, knowing that every hour will bring new strength, and every day will be a better day. Make *him* to know that *he* is not alone, for Thou art always with *him*. Give *him* now Thy peace which passes understanding and the courage not to give up, through Jesus Christ, who endured the cross, we pray. Amen.

EXTREME ILLNESS

Meditation: (Said to family if patient is not conscious.) The doctors are doing everything within their power to sustain the life of your loved one. Whatever the outcome be, we must be prepared to leave it in the hands of God. We have not given up hope of recovery, for where faith is alive, hope is alive. If the body is beyond repair, however, we must be prepared for God to take the soul, and believe that "though the outward man is wasting away, the inward man is being renewed."

Scripture: The Lord is my light and my salvation; whom shall I fear? The Lord is the stronghold of my life; of whom shall I be afraid? (*Psalm 27:1*).

Pastor's Prayer: O Thou, who art a refuge of the dis-tressed and the helper of the needy: Out of the depth of our helplessness we cry unto Thee, praying that Thou wilt give us such a sense of Thy presence as will comfort our hearts and make us feel that, whatever may come, Thou wilt work together for our good.

May this Thy child, who has been brought near to death, realize that Thine arms are around *him*. If, in harmony with Thy wise and merciful purposes, Thou canst raise *him* from *his* present estate and restore *his* health, our hearts will be filled with joy and thanksgiving; but if Thou dost see that it is best for *him* to pass into the unseen world, may we bow in humble recognition to Thy will, and may *he* have the consciousness of Thy presence with *him* as *he* "walks through the valley of the shadow." Grant, O merciful Father, that *he* may rise up out of the night of death into the light of that brighter day, and into the enjoyment of the "inheritance incorruptible, and undefiled, and that fadeth not away." Amen.[9]

PRAYERS FOR THE SICK

FOR REST

O God, I am weary with restlessness. Make me to be still. Make me to be at peace in my soul, and my muscles to give over their tension; make me to know that as I rest upon my bed, so I rest in Thee and in Thy support; in Thy peace I would abide all the days of my life; in Thy house would I lie down unto deep slumber as a guest rests after a weary journey; and I would dwell in the house of the Lord forever. Amen.[10]

FOR SLEEP

Eternal and Everlasting God, in the growing quietness of evening and the deepening shadows of the night, grant us sleep and rest. With the stilling of the day's doings, and the end of coming and going about us, make us to be sleepy with heavy eyes and tired limbs. As Thy creatures are lying down in the wood, as the bird is quiet in its nest . . . as the stream is still in its bed reflecting the great expanse of the stars above, may we in our sleep reflect our confidence in Thee, and our assurance in Thy constant peace. In our sleep give us that deeper communion of our souls with Thee which restoreth unto health. In His name. Amen.[11]

FOR COMPANIONSHIP OF THE SPIRIT

Eternal Father, Thou who art the companion of those who need Thee: Be Thou our companion. Pass with us through the valley of loneliness and stand with us beyond its turmoil. Stir us to find heaven in common things and friendliness in the commonplace. Make us to be friendly. In the weary hours of dark nights and the drudgery of slow turning days, we would remember Thee; when others forget us in their busy routine, Thou wilt not forget. Build Thou within us a new companionship, a companionship of the spirit. As the sea is to the ship, as the air is to the bird, so art Thou unto us in our meditation. So we would know Thee and Thy ways of working for the sake of Jesus. Amen.[12]

FOR UNDERSTANDING

O most merciful Father, Thou who art ever more willing to forgive than we are to ask, pardon our transgressions. In the lonely hours of forgetfulness we have been unmindful of Thee and of Thy commandments; O God forgive us, we pray. In our indifference we have been unfaithful to those we love, and to Him who didst open our eyes to Thee, Jesus Christ our Lord. As a child plays and is burned, as a child stumbles and falls, so we are hurt by our willfulness: Make us whole; give us strong limbs for walking, and strong wills in the places we are weak. Reward those we have hurt, and make us strong to reward them ourselves. We rejoice in the warmth of Thy affection and in the peace of Thy forgiveness. To Thee and to Jesus Christ, Thy Son, be honor and glory, world without end. Amen.[13]

FOR PATIENCE TO OVERCOME HANDICAP

O God of mercy, comfort us in our time of need; we are bowed down in our misfortune. We cling to Thee in our despair. Thou who art with us when we are lonely, Thou who dost forgive us when we are bitter, make us to have patience. We bless Thee for Christ who did suffer upon the cross, yet was He lifted above His suffering. Make us to know the meaning of the cross for ourselves. Our friend doth suffer handicap we know not why; make *him* to know that beyond the cross there is the resurrection, beyond the suffering of humility and imprisonment there is the newly won freedom of fortitude, patience and triumph. Make *him* to turn *his* suffering to Thy glory and the world will give praise for *his* devotion. In the name of Jesus. Amen.[14]

TO ACCEPT PAIN

Eternal God, whose days are without end, whose mercies are without number, we lift our minds to Thee in our stress: Make us to be still before Thee, make us to fasten our minds upon Thy quietness; give us strength, O God, for the task which is ours. Thy servant suffers from the pain. Give *him* strength to endure; make fast *his* mind in Thee and cause *him* to be strong in *his* endurance. Thou art the water of life; whosoever drinks of Thee shall not thirst. As the tired sheep drink of the cool water and rest beside the stream, so may we drink of Thy peace and rest in the coolness of Thy presence. In the name of that great shepherd of the sheep, Jesus Christ, our Lord. Amen.[15]

BEFORE AN OPERATION

Our Father, grant us Thy peace, Thou who dost wait upon us when we are restless and who dost grant us courage when we are fearful. Grant us quietness, grant us confidence, knowing that at this hour and in the days that are to follow we are in worthy and capable hands. Strengthen him who is to operate and those who are to serve as nurses; we give ourselves into Thy sustaining presence. "I will lift up mine eyes unto the hills. From whence cometh my help? My help cometh from the Lord, who made heaven and earth." From the sight of the hills and the strength of the Lord may we gather vision, patience and strength unto ourselves. As the shepherd guardeth his sheep, so wilt Thou guard this one now and in the days that are to follow. In the name of Jesus, Amen.[16]

WITH ONE BEYOND HEALING

God our Father, Thou hast promised that Thy grace is sufficient for our every need; so we come to Thee in prayer. Bless with the steadying power of faith this one who seems to be beyond healing, for whom the skill of man can do nothing more. Grant, we beseech Thee, the serenity which is certain that nothing in life or in death, in time or eternity, can separate *him* from Thee, through Jesus Christ, our Lord. Amen.

WITH ONE MENTALLY ILL

Father of mercies and God of all comfort: We commend to Thy fatherly goodness this one whose emotions are disturbed and whose mind is filled with tension.

O God, cheer *him* in time of melancholy; calm *him* in times of violence; clear *his* thinking in times of confusion. Protect *him* from doing harm to *himself* or others; and give understanding and patience to others that they may do no harm to *him*. O God, forgive what has been said or done in times of affliction. Restore hope where faith has grown weary. Confirm the evidences of recovery. Bless the endeavors of those who labor and pray on behalf of this Thy child, and bring us all to Thine everlasting Kingdom, through Jesus Christ our Lord. Amen.

WITH A SICK CHILD

O Lord, Jesus Christ, good Shepherd of the sheep, who dost gather the lambs with Thine arms and carry them in Thy bosom: We commit into Thy loving hands this child. Relieve *his* pain, guard *him* in all danger; restore unto *him* Thy gifts of gladness and strength, and raise *him* up to a life of service for Thee. Hear us, we beseech Thee, for Thy dear name's sake. Amen.[17]

Eternal God, Thou who dost bear us up in our travail, and who dost comfort us in our moments of weakness, be Thou with this one as *she* suffers. Grant *her* relief from this pain, and give *her* patience and fortitude to endure to the end. Wilt Thou give us peace in Thy presence. In the quiet of the evening may we come unto Thee, and in the still of the morning may we dwell in Thy presence. As Thy glory shineth in the morning sunrise may we reflect Thy presence by our faith, in the name of the Father, the Son, and the Holy Spirit. Amen.[18]

IN THE EVENING

Eternal Father, we lift up our eyes unto Thee in the quiet of the evening. As the birds of the fields seek Thee for shelter, as the ship sails upon the sea and comes to harbor, so do we come unto Thee and are comforted, knowing that underneath are Thine everlasting arms. Give us rest in the night and in sleep envelop us, and finally bring us unto eternal life. Now may the Lord Jesus be and abide with us in His grace, mercy, and fellowship. Amen.[19]

GENERAL PRAYERS FOR THE SICK

Heavenly Father, unto whom no experience of ours is trivial or unknown: Bless this hospital patient this day with strength to overcome weakness, courage to endure pain, faith to dispel fear, and peace to still anxiety, through Jesus Christ, the Good Physician. Amen.

O Thou who hast fashioned our bodies with marvelous recovery powers: Grant that those who treat the sick may have compassion and sympathy, wisdom, and skill. May Thy patient not demand more than *his* share of attention, and help *him* to be appreciative, considerate and cheerful. Thus, may this hospital be the scene of spiritual growth as well as physical healing. Amen.

AT THE TIME OF DEATH

For so great a peace we are eternally thankful, our Father. Thou hast been good to us. Wouldst Thou ease our weariness and give us eternal rest. O Thou, who hast brought this one through this earthly journey, may *she* now begin that which is without end, the new life in the new day. We commend *her* unto Thee; in the name of Him who doth bear us up in the hour of our great need, even Jesus Christ our Lord. Amen.

APPROPRIATE SCRIPTURE READINGS

CONFIDENCE IN GOD

The Lord is my shepherd, I shall not want; he makes me lie down in green pastures. He leads me beside still waters; he restores my soul. He leads me in paths of righteousness for his name's sake. Even though I walk through the valley of the shadow of death, I fear no evil; for thou art with me; thy rod and thy staff, they comfort me. Thou preparest a table before me in the presence of my enemies; thou anointest my head with oil, my cup overflows. Surely goodness and mercy shall follow me all the days of my life; and I shall dwell in the house of the Lord for ever (*Psalm 23*).

GOD AS MY FORTRESS

He who dwells in the shelter of the Most High, who abides in the shadow of the Almighty, will say to the Lord, "My refuge and my fortress; my God in whom I trust." For he will deliver you from the snare of the fowler and from the deadly pestilence; he will cover you with his pinions, and under his wings you will find refuge; his faithfulness is a shield and buckler (*Psalm 91:1-4*).

THE ETERNITY OF GOD

Lord, thou hast been our dwelling place in all generations. Before the mountains were brought forth, or ever thou hadst formed the earth and the world, from everlasting to everlasting thou art God (*Psalm 90:1, 2*).

MY STRENGTH COMETH FROM GOD

I lift up my eyes to the hills. From whence does my help come? My help comes from the Lord, who made heaven and earth. He will not let your foot be moved, he who keeps you will not slumber. Behold, he who keeps Israel will neither slumber nor sleep. The Lord is your keeper; the Lord is your shade on your right hand. The sun shall not smite you by day, nor the moon by night. The Lord will keep you from all evil; he will keep your life. The Lord will keep your going out and your coming in from this time forth and for evermore (*Psalm 121*).

RELEASE FROM WORRY

Therefore I tell you, do not be anxious about your life, what you shall eat or what you shall drink, nor about your body, what you shall put on. Is not life more than food, and the body more than clothing? Look at the birds of the air: they neither sow nor reap nor gather into barns, and yet your heavenly Father feeds them. Are you not of more value than they? And which of you by being anxious can add one cubit to his span of life? (*Matthew 6:25-27*).

FORGET TODAY'S CONCERN

And why are you anxious about clothing? Consider the lilies of the field, how they grow; they neither toil nor spin; yet I tell you, even Solomon in all his glory was not arrayed like one of these. But if God so clothes the grass of the field, which today is alive and tomorrow is thrown into the oven, will he not much more clothe you, O men of little faith? Therefore do not be anxious, saying, "What shall we eat?" or "What shall we drink?" or "What shall we wear?" For the Gentiles seek all these things; and your heavenly Father knows that you need them all. But seek first his kingdom and his righteousness, and all these things shall be yours as well. Therefore do not be anxious about tomorrow, for tomorrow will be anxious for itself. Let the day's own trouble be sufficient for the day (*Matthew 6:28-34*).

ASK AND RECEIVE

Ask, and it will be given to you; seek and you will find; knock, and it will be opened to you. For every one who asks receives, and he who seeks finds, and to him who knocks it will be opened (*Matthew 7:7, 8*).

UNTO THE WEARY AND CONTRITE

Come to me, all who labor and are heavy-laden, and I will give you rest. Take my yoke upon you, and learn from me; for I am gentle and lowly in heart, and you will find rest for your souls. For my yoke is easy, and my burden is light (*Matthew 11:28-30*).

ON FAITH

Then the disciples came to Jesus privately and said, "Why could we not cast it out?" He said to them, "Because of your little faith. For truly, I say to you, if you have faith as a grain of mustard seed, you will say to this mountain, 'Move hence to yonder place,' and it will move; and nothing will be impossible to you" (*Matthew 17:19, 20*).

X. Materials for Special Occasions

SPECIAL DAYS OF THE CHRISTIAN YEAR
CHRISTMAS SUNDAY

Call to Worship

Glory to God in the highest, and on earth peace among men with whom he is pleased! (*Luke 2:14*).

Invocation

O God of Love, who centuries ago blessed our earth in the form of Jesus Christ: With glad hearts we come to adore Thee, to rekindle our sense of wonder in Thy majestic ways, and to look to the Christ as our star of hope. Forbid that we should be preoccupied with lesser interests and transient pleasures, that no room is left for Him who is the King of kings and the Prince of Peace, even Jesus the Saviour of the world. Amen.

Scripture Lessons

Psalms: 89:1-7; 89:19-22, 24; 98; 103; 148.
Old Testament: Isaiah 2:2-5; 9:2-7.
New Testament: Matthew 1:18-25; 2:1-23. John 1:1-34. Titus 2:11; 3:15. Hebrews 1.

Christmas Litany

Leader: For the life of Jesus Christ, through whom Thou hast revealed Thy love to us,

Response: We praise Thy name, O God.

Leader: For our share in the selfishness which rules our every day, the prejudices and suspicions which divide men, the love of unworthy things which cheapens life, and the indifference which allows evils contrary to Thy revealed will to go unchecked,

Response: Forgive us, Dear Lord.

Leader: May a new birth of Christ's spirit come into our hearts that our minds might be purified, our affections kindled, our compassion for the suffering quickened, our service made more generous, and our zeal for righteousness and peace more intense,

Response: We implore Thee, through Jesus Christ our Lord. Amen.

Pastor's Christmas Prayer

God of Grace and God of Glory: Before Thy throne we humble ourselves, seeking forgiveness for our feeble efforts to understand the magnitude and meaning of Christ's birth and for our indifference to that for which He lived and died. For the trifling selfishness that fills our time with other things, our mind with other thoughts, our hearts with other loves, and the rooms of our lives with lesser guests until Christ is crowded out, we plead Thy forgiveness, O God. At this Christmas season, give us the disposition to let Christ be born anew within each of our lives, creating in us a new outlook, new serenity, firmer convictions, and a new spirit.

May the spirit of Jesus help heal the wounds and scars left by misunderstanding, betrayal of trust, and evil deeds. Help those who have been wronged to forgive and those who have wronged to repent. Cleanse us of ambitions that have no rightful place in the Christian heart. Turn our eyes to men and women whose hopes have turned to ashes; our ears to the cries of children denied proper chances in life; and our energies to those caught in complex circumstances.

We pray for love and goodness to those who have no Christmas—for boys and girls whose hands press against store windows while their eyes devour the glories they can never touch. We pray penitence for those who think they are having Christmas, but have none because of hearts torn by hate, twisted by prejudice, crippled by pride, and betrayed by deceit. We pray for steppingstones to higher things for children in whose homes the candles have been put out by fear and pestilence, and for the darkened millions who go to bed hungry. We pray for faith, patience, and consolation to those whose homes are empty with the passing of loved ones. Tie these cares to our hearts, O God. Amen.

PALM SUNDAY

Call to Worship

Lift up your heads, O gates! and be lifted up, O ancient doors! that the King of glory may come in. Who is this King of glory? The Lord of hosts, he is the King of glory (*Psalm 24:9-10*).

Invocation

Messiah of the ages, whose spirit is forever seeking entrance into our world's life, and whose church ever seeks to extend Thine empire over human hearts: We would open now the doors of our hearts to Thee. Forbid that we should hail Thee as Master when all men speak well of

Thee, and then deny Thee in the lonely hour of rejection. Grant us in this hour glimpses of service wherein we can hasten the consummation of Thy Kingdom in which Christ shall be the only King. Amen.

Scripture Lessons

Psalms: 8; 15; 16:6-11; 24; 29; 102:1, 8-12.
Old Testament: Jeremiah 7:1-11; 18:1-14.
New Testament: Matthew 21:23-46. Mark 15:16-20. Luke 19:29-44. John 19:1-37.

Palm Sunday Litany

Leader: Behold thy King cometh. In His days shall the righteous flourish, and abundance of peace so long as the moon endureth. He shall have dominion from sea to sea, and from the river unto the ends of the earth.

Response: Blessed is He that cometh in the name of the Lord.

Leader: God has highly exalted Him, and bestowed on Him a name which is above every name; that at the name of Jesus every knee should bow in heaven and on earth and under the earth, and every tongue confess that Jesus Christ is Lord, to the glory of God the Father.

Response: Enter into His gates with thanksgiving and into His courts with praise.

Pastor's Palm Sunday Prayer

O God, whose dearly beloved Son was greeted by the crowd on Olivet with Hallelujahs, but who in that same week was mocked as He went lonely to the Cross: Forbid that our praise to Him should be in words alone. Help us, we pray, to keep the road open for Him into our hearts; let Him not find in us another crucifixion—but rather love and loyalty in which His Kingdom may be established ever more.

O Christ, King of the Universe, who dost forever ride up to the gates of human lives: Open our hearts to Thy love, Thy light, Thy spirit, that we may receive Thee as our King and never reject Thee. Enter our cities, take captive our homes, cleanse our churches of ugliness, pollution, and indifference; drive out those who traffic upon human souls; reign, O Master, till all injustice, all evil, all smallness is dethroned and destroyed.

Merciful Father: Pardon us who often close the gates of our lives against the entrance of Christ's spirit; forgive our love of self which does not allow Him to lead us in a larger life; deliver us from ambitions and rivalries that will not allow Him to lead our homes, cities and nation.

Save us from the hypocrisy that sings *Hosanna* in the church and cries *Crucify* in the market place. Save us from the sham that praises with lips but betrays in deeds. Deliver us from the treason that boasts loyalty in the upper room but makes cowardly denial in the judgment halls.

When the palms have withered, the songs are dead, and the streets empty, may we find ourselves at the end of life's little day still with Thee. Amen.[1]

THURSDAY BEFORE EASTER

Call to Worship

I am the living bread which came down from heaven; if any one eats of the bread, he will live for ever; and the bread which I shall give for the life of the world is my flesh (*John 6:51*).

Invocation

O God, who canst guide our feet into the sanctuary of Thy presence: Make ready, we beseech Thee, our hearts to receive the sacrament of that love whereby Thy Son hath redeemed us; through the same Jesus Christ our Lord. Amen.[2]

Scripture Lessons

Psalms: 23; 24; 34; 56; 65.
Old Testament: Isaiah 50:4-11; 55. Zechariah 9:9-14.
New Testament: Matthew 26:17-30. Mark 14:17-26. Luke 23:1-49. John 13:1-15. I Corinthians 11:17-34.

Communion Litany

Leader: If we have forgotten Thee in the distractions of the workaday world and lost the sense of Thy presence in the crowded hours of our days, if we have forsaken Thine altars and turned our hearts from worship,

Response: May we remember Thee, O Lord.

Leader: If Thy service has made demands upon us which we have been slow to grant and the tasks of Thy Kingdom have found us reluctant to assume them,

Response: May we remember Thee, O Lord.

Leader: As we sit together in the gracious fellowship of this communion hour, with hearts that are one in aspiration and in hope . . . may we accept the Master's commandment,

Response: This do in remembrance of me.[3]

Pastor's Communion Prayer

O Thou who hast consecrated for us a new and living way, even Jesus Christ our Lord: Grant us who are here met, so to partake of this bread and this cup that our hearts and lives may be truly yielded to the sway of His spirit. And here we offer and present unto Thee, O Lord, ourselves, our souls and bodies, to be a reasonable, holy and living sacrifice unto Thee. Now, as we commemorate His last supper with His disciples, and His offering of Himself in the sacrifice of the cross, we humbly beseech Thee to grant Thy Holy Spirit, and to sanctify this bread and cup, that they may become unto us symbols of the body that was broken and of the blood that was shed for us. May they beget in us penitent hearts and a quickening faith, and may we receive this holy sacrament; through Jesus Christ our Lord. Amen.[4]

GOOD FRIDAY

Call to Worship

Surely he has borne our griefs and carried our sorrows . . . he was wounded for our transgressions, he was bruised for our iniquities; upon him was the chastisement that made us whole; and with his stripes we are healed. . . . Let us then with confidence draw near to the throne of grace, that we may receive mercy and find grace to help in time of need (*Isaiah 53:4, 5; Hebrews 4:16*).

Invocation

Almighty and most merciful God, whose will is that all men should be saved, and who didst give Thy Son our Lord Jesus Christ to be the propitiation for the sins of the whole world: We bow in adoration before Thy throne and praise Thee for this Thine unspeakable gift. Amen.[5]

Scripture Lessons

Psalm: 22.

Old Testament: Isaiah 53:1-12; 63:1-9.

New Testament: Matthew 27:33-55. Mark 15:16-41 Luke 23:26-49. John 19:1-37.

Good Friday Litany

Leader: All loving and gracious God, who dost permit us to draw nigh to Thee: Dispose our hearts aright, that we may lift up prayer and praise to Thee, trusting not in our well-deserving, but in Thy great mercy; through Thine only begotten Son, Jesus Christ.

Response: Bow down Thine ear, O Lord, and answer us; for we are poor and needy.

Leader: Comfort the soul of Thy servant; for Thou, Lord, art gracious and ever ready to forgive.

Response: Bestow upon us Thy lovingkindness and Thy tender mercies, and heal us with Thy holy presence.

Leader: That in the life of Jesus Christ our Lord, born of a woman and bearing in Himself the temptations of mortal flesh, Thou hast revealed Thine immeasurable love to us,

Response: We bless Thee, O Lord.

Leader: That in His life and death He did not refuse to share the lot of common man, but humbled Himself and became obedient to death, even the death of the cross,

Response: We bless Thee, O Lord.

Leader: That Thou didst not leave Thy Holy One to see corruption, but didst raise Him by the right hand of Thy power, to be to us for evermore the promise of eternal life,

Response: We bless Thee, O Lord.

Leader: Grant that this day of holy memorial, when we recall His dying agony and His redeeming love, may be to us, His disciples, for the renewal of our faith and the sanctification of our lives,

Response: Hear us, good Lord.

Leader: For the forgiveness of our sins and for the cleansing of our hearts,

Response: We bless Thee, O Lord.

Leader: For that preparation of heart and mind that shall enable us to receive Thy Holy Spirit,

Response: We pray Thee, O Lord.[6]

Pastor's Good Friday Prayer

Eternal God, our Father, who didst send Thy Son to be the Saviour of the world: We wait before Thee in the shadows of the cross where He made the supreme sacrifice that lost men might find their way back to Thee. We confess that the sins which killed Him often beseige our own hearts. We see ourselves in the varied company around Him on Golgotha. We know the mood of fear, jealousy, hatred, and love of power. Search us, O God, and reveal to us our evil ways that in full surrender to Thee we may be cleansed of all that corrupts our souls and separates us from Thee. Forbid that on this day of His great agony we should join the mob that watched Him there in morbid humor and pagan cruelty. Deliver us from the passive curiosity that waits a sign and the hypocrisy that joins the crowd to hide its emptiness. May Thy Spirit find us today where we really are in our human frailty, our lagging loyalty, and our lack of faith. May the Light that overcomes the darkness touch the unseen depths of our hearts and expel all cowardice and unworthy motive. May He who came to make all things new begin in us now, and continue with each passing day, that work of redemption which shall give us the right to share in His resurrection and make this earth at last the heaven for which He taught us to pray. Amen.[7]

EASTER SUNDAY

Call to Worship

O the depth of the riches and wisdom and knowledge of God! How unsearchable are his judgments and how inscrutable his ways! . . . For from him and through him and to him are all things. To him be glory forever (*Romans 11:33, 36*).

Invocation

O Thou who makest the stars and turnest the shadow of death into the morning: On this day of days we meet to render to Thee, our Lord and King, the tribute of our praise; for the resurrection of the springtime, for the everlasting hopes that rise within the human heart, and for the gospel which hath brought life and immortality to light. Receive our thanksgiving, reveal Thy presence, and send forth into our hearts the Spirit of the risen Christ.[8]

Scripture Lessons

Psalms: 50:1-7, 23; 97:1, 2, 4-12; 111; 115; 116:1-9; 118:1-7a, 17.

Old Testament: Isaiah 25:1-9. Ezekiel 37:9-14.

New Testament: Matthew 27:57—28:20. Mark 15:42—16:20. Luke 23:50—24:18. John 19:38—20:18. I Corinthians 15:12-20, 53-57. Revelation 1:10-18.

Easter Litany

Leader: From the dust of vainly traveled highways and the weariness of almost forgotten hopes,

Response: Lift up our eyes to Thee, O Lord.

Leader: From the mysteries of evil, and pain, and sorrow, and from the dark records of history and tradition,

Response: Lift up our eyes to Thee, O Lord.

Leader: From the depths of sin, the limitations of our vision, the failures of our will, the littleness of our spiritual experience,

Response: Lift up our eyes to Thee, O Lord.

Leader: That we may know life with its eternal setting and become new creatures with minds set on things above,

Response: Grant us the victory, we pray.

Leader: That we may transform every defeat into triumph, every opposition into a way of help, and every sacrifice into a new attainment,

Response: Grant us the victory, we pray.[9]

Pastor's Easter Prayer

Righteous and ever-living God, whose Son on this day didst shatter the power of death, bringing life and immortality to light: We worship Thee. On this day of all days in humanity's history, assist us that we fail not in low aim or dull sensitiveness to its high significance. Intensify our feelings that already are athrob with emotions stirred by Thee and the eternal suggestions of this day. Give us the joy of the resurrection that turned night into light and mourning into laughter, to lighten up our too frequently drab lives. Give us the power of the resurrection, which broke the reign of death, to shatter every ancient tyranny that entombs Thy people: The intrigues of war, the subtlety of highly vested interests, contemptuous racial pride, and ambitious self-seekers. Give us the victory of Easter that turned a cross into a resurrection, and made the one-time symbol of shame the sign of Thy conquering hosts, to capture spiritual triumph from our worst material defeats, to make sickness a refining ministry to character, to transform tragedy into faith, and all bitterness into love. Give us the peace of the resurrection that calmed the terrorized hearts of Thy children of old. Until the day dawns grant us brave hearts and constant spirits; and ever to Thee be praise and glory, world without end. Amen.

PENTECOST SUNDAY

Call to Worship

You shall receive power when the Holy Spirit has come upon you; and you shall be my witnesses in Jerusalem and in all Judea and Samaria and to the end of the earth (*Acts 1:8*).

Invocation

O Spirit of the Living God, breathe upon this assembled company Thy gracious power. Come to us as long ago like a flame of fire to burn out our moral pollution so that to the core of self we may be clean. Come to us as a rushing, mighty wind, scattering the mists of our doubt, stirring our spirits to health and action, sweeping aside the fears that have held us in captivity. Come to disturb our apathy. Come, Holy Spirit, come.[10]

Scripture Lessons

Psalms: 47:1, 2, 4-9; 67; 96:1-7; 96:7-13; 139:1-12, 17, 18.

Old Testament: Daniel 7:9-14.

New Testament: John 3:1-21, 31-36. Acts 2:1-15, 22-24, 36-47, 14-42. Romans 8:1-17, 18-39.

Pentecost Litany

Leader: Spirit of God, Spirit of Christ, Holy Spirit the Comforter, Spirit of truth, Spirit of holiness, Spirit of promise,

Response: Hear us, we beseech Thee.

Leader: That Thy gifts may be stirred up in all those who have been called into Thy church, that the world may be convicted by Thee of its sin, that there may speedily increase amongst us Thy Kingdom which is righteousness and peace,

Response: Hear us, we beseech Thee.

Leader: That Thou wilt teach us how to pray, that our mortal bodies may be quickened by Thy dwelling in us, that we may walk no more after the flesh but after the spirit,

Response: Hear us, O Holy Spirit of God.

Pastor's Pentecost Prayer

O Thou of infinite power, who gavest birth to Thy church, who by Thy Spirit dost renew, illumine, refresh, and sanctify our souls: We worship Thee. Thou hast given hope to the fearful, strength to the weak, light to the doubting, and salvation to the lost.

In these quiet moments that haunt the mind, we acknowledge to Thee that we have not been what we ought, nor done what we should. We remember times when we have sown hatred instead of love, disturbance instead of peace, impatience instead of longsuffering, evil instead of goodness. We have talked when we should have been silent, and we have been silent when we should have witnessed. We have spent money when it was foolish, and have been greedy when we should have been generous. O God of mercy, forgive our ways, and illumine us with understanding to know what we ought to do and the commitment to do it.

On this day of Pentecost, once more make Thy church powerful with Thy Holy Spirit. After uneventful days and unmarked years disturb its lethargy, give it a new passion, unite its division, that it might redeem the world of its warring, godless ways, seek men and women hungry for life, challenge injustice that exploits innocent victims, and bring Thy love to all men everywhere, in the name of Jesus Christ. Amen.

REFORMATION SUNDAY

Call to Worship

Therefore, since we are surrounded by so great a cloud of witnesses, let us also lay aside every weight, and sin which clings so closely . . . looking to Jesus the pioneer and perfecter of our faith, who for the joy that was set before him endured the cross, despising the shame, and is seated at the right hand of the throne of God (*Hebrews 12:1, 2*).

Invocation

O God of truth, holiness and justice: We thank Thee for the moral and spiritual reformers who from time to time purified religious abuses, restored Christian principles, and by whose ardor and sacrifices we have the privilege of free worship in a free land.

Forgive careless indifference to our heritage, the divisions and selfishness which injure Thee. Revive in us this day a passion for truth, a sincere desire for brotherhood, and a dedication to carry on this unfinished reformation for freedom and unity through Jesus Christ. Amen.

Scripture Lessons

Psalms: 46; 125.

Old Testament: Jeremiah 31:31-35. Habakkuk 2:1-4, 18-20.

New Testament: John 8:23-36. Romans 1:14-17; 3:20-24. Galatians 3:6-11, 23-28.

Reformation Litany

Leader: Thus saith the Lord, If my people, who are called by my name, shall humble themselves, and pray, and seek my face, and turn from their wicked ways; then will I hear from heaven, and will forgive their sin, and will heal their land,

Response: Lord, be merciful to us.

Leader: For our divisions within the household of faith, our willful misunderstanding of each other's positions, our unwillingness to admit our faults, our blindness to the virtues of others, our insincerity in worship, our lack of zeal for truth, our complacency and self-righteousness, our lack of concern for those living without Christ,

Response: O Lord, forgive us.

Unison: Make us, O God, worthy of Thy church, and make Thy church worthy of Thy Christ.

Pastor's Reformation Prayer

O Thou who art the source of freedom: On this Reformation Sunday, we recall in humble gratitude those brave souls of past years, who dared danger, hardship, and persecution that they might win for themselves and for the world liberty of conscience and freedom in worship. Thou didst guide them to plant upon these shores the seeds of intellectual freedom and moral earnestness, whose harvest is our great republic. May their devotion to truth, heroic spirit, loyalty to Thee, and love of liberty abide always in us.

Forgive us, our Father, for betraying our heritage, for loving luxury and not the sacrifice of courageous witness, for accepting the conclusions of others without personal investigation, for establishing churches that compete with one another, for being so liberal that we have no commitments, and so negative that we fail to be creative. O Lord, in these confused times, raise up wise and faithful men with prophetic voices, who will see below the surface of our lives. Quicken us in conscience, disturb our lethargy, reclaim Thy priority that the church may fulfill its mission for such an hour, to the glory of Jesus Christ. Amen.

UNIVERSAL BIBLE SUNDAY

Call to Worship

These are written that you may believe that Jesus is the Christ, the Son of God, and that believing you may have life in his name (*John 20:31*). O land, land, land, hear the word of the Lord! (*Jeremiah 22:29*).

Invocation

Almighty and most merciful God, who has given the Bible to be the revelation of Thy great love to man, and of Thy power and will to serve him: Grant that our study of it may not be made in vain by the carelessness of our hearts, but that by it we may be confirmed in penitence, lifted to hope, made strong to serve, and above all, filled with the true knowledge of Thee and of Thy Son Jesus Christ. Amen.

Scripture Lessons

Psalms: 19; 119:27-112; 147

Old Testament: Deuteronomy 5:6-24. II Kings 22:3-11; 23:1-3. Ezra 8:1-8.

New Testament: Matthew 5:13-20. Luke 8:4-15. James 1:5-27.

Bible Litany

Leader: For this Book, the inspiration of all our Christian education which nurtures children with spiritual food, which inspires youth to victorious living, and sustains age in faith and works,

Response: We give Thee thanks, O God.

Leader: For this Book, a standard for the Christian church, whereby she may be corrected in error, healed in her divisions, and made one in Christ so that the world may believe.

Response: We give Thee thanks, O God.

Leader: For this Book, with its consolation in sorrow, hope in discouragement, light in darkness, truth in error, faith in doubt, victory in temptation, peace in turmoil, and strength in every need,

Response: We give Thee thanks, O God.

Leader: For this Book, the precious heritage of all mankind, a lamp unto our feet and a light unto our path, from youth to old age, in sickness and health, in plenty and in want, until the eternal Day breaks and the shadows flee away,

Response: We give Thee thanks, O God.[11]

Pastor's Bible Prayer

O God of life, grant that we may see in all creation Thy power which upholds us; in the pages of the Bible Thy wisdom that seeks us; in the face of Jesus Christ Thy love which saves us; and in the Holy Spirit, a new life which enthralls us.

Make us sensitive to Thee, just now, who are closer than breathing, and nearer than hands and feet.

Grant, O Lord, that beginning today we may seek more diligently the deep wisdom of the Bible, and come to understand it better. Make it a spur to our weakness, a trumpet call to our flagging will, a cleansing rebuke to our sins. Let it reveal to us the glory and goodness and the beauty of Thee. Fuse its principles into our everyday living and decisions; thread its spirit into our thoughts; empower us through its poetry. Through the rise and fall of nations, teach us its eternal truth that righteousness exalteth a nation but sin is a reproach to any people. Enlarge the purposes for which we live in the vision of a new and better age for this our world. Reveal with renewed clarity the wisdom, power, and salvation of the One in whom we find Thyself, even Jesus Christ. Amen.

SPECIAL SUNDAYS OF THE CIVIL YEAR
NEW YEAR'S SUNDAY

Call to Worship

O give thanks to the Lord, for he is good; for his steadfast love endures for ever (*Psalm 136:1*).

Invocation

O Thou who art from everlasting to everlasting, by whose mercy we have come to the gateway of another year:

We lift our hearts in thanksgiving to Thee. Replenish us with heavenly grace at the beginning of this year, that we may be enabled to accept all its duties, to perform all its labors, to welcome all its mercies, to meet all its trials, and to advance through all it holds in store, with cheerful courage and confident faith, in Jesus Christ, our Lord. Amen.

Scripture Lessons

Psalms: 1; 4; 15; 23; 27; 39:1-13; 91; 115.

Old Testament: Exodus 20:1-17. Deuteronomy 11:1-17, 18-20, 26-28. Proverbs 3:11-20. Joshua 3:1-6, 9, 10a, 11.

New Testament: Matthew 10:5-42. Mark 1:21-45. Luke 3:1-23; 6:20-49. John 1:35—2:12.

New Year's Litany

Leader: O God our Father: For Thy providence which had led us through another year, for Thy lovingkindness which has been beyond our deserving, for the good hopes and precious memories, for courage and strength given us through Thy Spirit, for the protection of our homes, for the measure of success Thou hast granted to our labors, for the grace and saving health we have received through Christ our Saviour,

Response: We give Thee thanks, O God.

Leader: Forgive us wherein we have wasted our time or misused our gifts. Forgive us wherein we have excused our own wrongdoing or evaded our responsibilities. Forgive us that so little of Thy love has reached others through us. Forgive us wherein we have cherished the things that divide us from others and wherein we have been thoughtless in our judgments, hasty in condemnation, or reluctant to forgive,

Response: Have mercy upon us and forgive us, O Lord.

Unison: Have mercy upon us, O God, according to Thy

lovingkindness. According to the multitude of Thy tender mercies, blot out our transgressions. Wash us thoroughly from our iniquity, and cleanse us from our sin. Create in us a clean heart, O God, and renew a right spirit within us.

Pastor's New Year's Prayer

O Thou who art the same yesterday, today and forever: Times change and we change, but Thou art constant in love for Thy children and ceaseless in giving of Thyself. So our first thoughts in this new year are of Thee, our first words are in praise of Thee, our first impulse is to love Thee, our first action is to worship Thee. Accept now the meditations of our hearts.

We acknowledge before Thee our faults and failures of the past year, and plead for Thy forgiveness. For every evil thought which our minds have welcomed; for the hard, harsh words we have spoken; for the duties we have shirked; for being quick to see the evil in our comrades and slow to recognize the wrong in ourselves, we ask Thy forgiveness.

Teach us, our Father, that real happiness is more in our disposition than in our position. Give us friends who love us for what we are, even though they know us at our worst.

We pray for those who know not where to lay their heads; for those who in beds cannot sleep for pain or worry; for those who work too little and so know not the joy of labor; for those who work too much and leave no time for the joys of leisure; for those puzzled about life's injustices, for missionaries of the cross in lonely places.

Grant, O Lord, that when this worship is over, we shall not let Thy praises end, lest we spend this year in forgetfulness of Thee. From this hour may Thy power and grace keep us trustful in our words, humble and honorable in our wishes, industrious and intelligent in our work, and loyal and dependable in our devotion, that Christ may live in us and abide with us. Amen.

Call to Worship

Have we not all one father? Has not one God created us? Why then are we faithless to one another, profaning the convenant of our fathers? . . . There is one body and one Spirit, just as you were called to the one hope that belongs to your call, one Lord, one faith, one baptism, one God and Father of us all, who is above all and through all and in all (*Malachi 2:10; Ephesians 4:4-7*).

Invocation

Almighty God, who art our Heavenly Father: Thou hast made us one in our need of Thee; one in our desire for Thy fellowship; one in our common hope of life everlasting; unite us we beseech Thee in holy worship. So illumine ourselves to ourselves and so transform our evil ways that we might ascend to Thy holy will, and go forth united in common endeavors for Thee, through Jesus Christ. Amen.

Scripture Lessons

Psalms: 9; 10; 67; 96; 133.
Old Testament: Genesis 44:18-34; 45:1-15. Amos 5. Proverbs 1:1-19.
New Testament: Luke 10:25-37. John 15. Romans 12. I Corinthians 12:1-27. I John 2; 3; 4. Galatians 3.

Brotherhood Litany

Leader: How good and how pleasant it is for brothers to dwell together in unity. It is like the precious ointment upon the head. It is like the dew of Hermon, or the dew upon the mountains of Lebanon, giving fragrance, and refreshment, and the blessings of God forevermore. God hath made of one blood all nations and people to dwell on the earth.

Response: Make real to us, O God, that all men are brothers, through our divine brother, Christ Jesus.

Leader: There is no difference between Jew and Greek, male or female, bond or free.

Response: Make real to us, O God, that all men are brothers, through Christ Jesus our Lord.

Leader: This is the message that ye heard from the beginning that we should love one another.

Response: Make real to us, O God, that all men are brothers.

Leader: He who loveth God shall love his brother also.

Response: Make real to us, O God, that all men are brothers.

Leader: He who loveth not his brother whom he hath seen, how can he love God whom he hath not seen?

Response: Make real to us, O God, that all men are brothers.

Leader: Do ye to others as ye would that they should do to you.

Response: Make real to us, O God, that all men are brothers.

Leader: Inasmuch as ye have done it to one of the least of these, my brethren, ye have done it to me.

Response: Make real to us, O God, that all men are brothers through our divine brother, Jesus Christ.

Leader: Go into all the world and preach the gospel to the whole creation. He who believes and is baptized will be saved.

Response: Thanks be to Thee, O God, our Father that all peoples at home and in all the world, of every race, creed and color are brothers for whom Christ died.[12]

Pastor's Brotherhood Prayer

O Thou who art the God of all the world and the Divine Father of all mankind: We are grateful that Thou art no respecter of persons. As we meditate upon Thy love, Thy truth, and Thy will as revealed in Jesus Christ, may we be re-inspired and re-convicted with the ideas that cannot be argued down nor shot down, but which can bring a peaceful and orderly and just climate in which all Thy children can live happily. We confess to the many injustices and prejudices of which we are guilty. Remove from us all unchristian attitudes. Lift us above all that alienates and separates the human family. Help us to treat all men as brothers, acknowledging their rights, recognizing their differences, but having regard for their welfare.

We are grateful to Thee for the advancement of brotherhood among men; for the wider diffusion of opportunities; for the brave, courageous men of principle who have withstood ridicule for principle, safety for conviction, and loss of popularity and position for persons. Endue them with Thy Holy Spirit and through Jesus Christ enable us to strive in this world for that fellowship of kindred spirits to which we look forward in the heavenly Kingdom, in the name of our Saviour. Amen.

Call to Worship

Therefore come out from them, and be separate from them, says the Lord (*II Corinthians 6:17, 18*).

Invocation

Eternal God, Father of the human family, we worship Thee through voices raised in song, through instruments of praise, through the stillness of silence, through the humility of a contrite spirit, and through Jesus Christ our Lord. Amen.

Scripture Lessons

Psalms: 102; 127; 128.

Old Testament: I Samuel 1:9-20, 24-28. II Kings 4:18-37. Proverbs 31:10-31.

New Testament: Matthew 15:21-28. Luke 2:39-55. II Timothy 1:2-9.

Christian Family Life Litany

Leader: O God, our heavenly Father, whose goodness loved us into life, and whose mercies never fail: We commend to Thee all who have a place in our hearts and sympathies; all who are joined to us by the sacred ties of kindred, friendship, and love,

Response: We beseech Thee to hear us, O Lord.

Leader: Grant unto us a revival of the simplicity and purity of home life; may parents bring up their children in the nurture and admonition of the Lord, and children love and reverence their parents; stir up in the young a zeal for whatever things are beautiful and true and good, that they may bravely witness for Thee; and keep the hearts

of the aged fresh with sweet affections and quiet trust, that
at their eventide there may be light,

Response: We beseech Thee to hear us, O Lord.

Leader: For the careless and the wayward that they may
be delivered from the bonds of iniquity; for all who are
beset by passionate temptations that Thy mercy may be
their salvation; and for all who are lonely and sad in the
midst of others' joy that they may know God as their
Friend and Comforter,

Response: We beseech Thee to hear us, O Lord.[13]

Pastor's Mother's Day Prayer

O God, who didst create mothers to a high and holy
duty: We thank Thee for the example of the beautiful life
of the mother of the Saviour and for the example of Christ's
devotion to His mother. Open the eyes of mothers everywhere that they may see not only the drudgery of house-
work and the exacting demands of rearing children, but
especially the blessed privilege that is theirs in the opportunity of making the next generation more Christian and
in bringing little ones to Thee and to the Saviour.
Where we as children have failed to heed the Christian
counsel of our parents, or have refused to walk the Christian way they showed us how to walk, forgive us for Jesus'
sake. Where we as parents have failed to teach our children of Thee as a loving Father, of Christ as a forgiving
Saviour, and of Thy will, forgive us for Jesus' sake. Comfort the parents whose hearts are grieved by wayward children, and let such children quickly see the folly of their
ways. Let mothers and children who are separated find
comfort in the knowledge that Thou dost watch over them
all. Bless all mothers richly and let them be a blessing to
their children; through Jesus Christ our Lord. Amen.[14]

MEMORIAL DAY SUNDAY

Call to Worship

The righteous live for ever, and in the Lord is their reward and the care of them with the most High. Therefore shall they receive the crown of royal dignity and the diadem of beauty from the Lord's hand (*The Wisdom of Solomon 5:15-16*).

Invocation

Eternal God, Father of our spirits: We rejoice in all who have faithfully lived and triumphantly died. We give Thee thanks for all blessed memories and all enduring hopes; for the ties that bind us to the unseen world; for all the heroic dead who encompass us like a cloud of witnesses. We pray that we who have entered into the heritage of their heroism and self-sacrifice may so honor their memory and so preserve and further their high purposes that the nation which they defended may stand in all coming years for righteousness and peace, through Jesus Christ, their Lord and ours. Amen.[15]

Scripture Lessons

Psalms: 44:1-4, 6, 7, 20-26; 46; 77:1-20; 137:1-6; 145:10-21.

Old Testament: Isaiah 52:3-12.

New Testament: John 14:1-15. II Timothy 1:1—2:12. Hebrews 11:17—12:2. I Peter 1. Revelation 7:9-17; 21:1-7; 21:23—22:5.

Memorial Litany

Leader: For the land of our birth, with all its chartered liberties, for all the wonder of our country's story,

Response: We praise Thee, O God.

Leader: For leaders in nation and state, and those who in days past and in these present times have labored for the commonwealth; for those who in all times and places have been true and brave, and in the world's common ways have lived upright lives and ministered to their fellows; for those who served their country in her hour of need, and especially for those who gave even their lives,

Response: We praise Thee, O God.

Unison: O Almighty God and merciful Father, whose nature and whose name is Love: As we give Thee thanks for the courage and the strength vouchsafed to these Thy servants, we would remember before Thee those who mourn them as their kindred. Look in mercy upon them; and as this day brings them memories of those whom they have lost, may it also bring them consolation from Thee, quickening in them the sense of communion with the world unseen, and confirming their assurance of that day when Thou shalt restore to them their own in the very presence of our Lord and Saviour Jesus Christ. Amen.[16]

Pastor's Memorial Day Prayer

God of our fathers, who hast made us the heirs of faithful men of all generations who have given themselves to great endeavors and made life nobler because they have walked its ways: We thank Thee for every memory that enriches life with high ideals and great purposes. We thank Thee for all who have loved this land which we love, who have been eager to establish freedom and justice within our borders, and have given themselves for the fulfillment of their longings. We thank Thee for all who have laboured for a friendly world, free from hatred and bitterness, and have spent themselves in their pursuit of peace. We thank

Thee for all who in school or laboratory, in church or state, in home or industry have sought to fill life with the mind of Christ. We thank Thee for those dear to us, forgotten by the world but still living in our hearts, who rest from their labours, and whose works do follow them. Make this day of memory a day of peace through our faith that they live with us in Thy love. Grant that though dead they may still speak to us, bidding us further every cause of righteousness and truth which they have served, and assuring us that they without us shall not be made perfect. Amen.[17]

INDEPENDENCE DAY SUNDAY

Call to Worship

Blessed is the nation whose God is the Lord, the people whom he has chosen as his heritage (*Psalm 33:12*).

Invocation

O eternal God, through whose mighty power our fathers won their liberties of old: Grant, we beseech Thee, that we and all the people of this land may have grace to maintain these liberties in righteousness and peace; through Jesus Christ our Lord. Amen.[18]

Scripture Lessons

Psalms: 18:1-20; 33:12-22; 48:1-3, 7-14; 107:1-8; 121; 122; 124; 146.

Old Testament: Deuteronomy 4:1-14. Isaiah 26:1-4, 7-8, 12.

New Testament: John 8:31-36. Romans 12:1-13. Galatians 5. I Timothy 2; 3. Hebrews 10:32; 11:16; 12:28. I Peter 2.

National Litany

Leader: O God, our Lord, who hast made us one nation out of many peoples: Amid our diversities of race and class and tradition, unite us in a common love of freedom and in high ambitions.

Response: Help us to establish our land in every righteous way. Maintain our generation in liberty and the struggle for justice and good will.

Leader: O God, remember not the offenses of Thy people; deal not with us after our sins, neither reward us according to our wickedness.

Response: From the love of ease, blindness of heart, and presumptuous pride, save us, O Lord.

Leader: From class hatred, racial antagonisms, the seeking of self advantage and forgetfulness of the general good, save Thy people, O Lord.

Unison: Teach us, O Lord, to cooperate effectively with other nations, to work for the abolition of war, the establishment of international law, and whatever else may pertain to the general good.

Pastor's Independence Day Prayer

Grant us, O God, a vision of our land, fair as she might be; a land of justice, where none shall prey on others; a land of plenty, where vice and poverty shall cease to fester; a land of brotherhood, where success shall be founded on service, and honor be given to worth alone; a land of peace where order need no longer rest on force, but on the love of all for their land, the great mother of the common life and welfare. Hear Thou, O Lord, the silent prayer of all our hearts, as in city, town, and village we pledge our time and strength, and thought to hasten the

day of her coming beauty and righteousness; through Jesus
Christ our Lord. Amen.[19]

LABOR DAY SUNDAY

Call to Worship

[Jesus said] Come to me, all who labor and are heavy-
laden, and I will give you rest. Take my yoke upon you,
and learn from me; for I am gentle and lowly in heart,
and you will find rest for your souls. For my yoke is easy,
and my burden is light (*Matthew 11:28-30*).

Invocation

O Thou who workest ever, but weariest not: We thank
Thee for the sacredness of toil, and seek Thy favor on our
labor that we may ever keep alive our kinship with Thee,
in the name of the Master Workman we pray. Amen.

Scripture Lessons

Psalms: 8; 43; 72:1-4, 7, 8; 112:1-7, 9; 124; 147.
Old Testament: Nehemiah 2:1-18.
New Testament: Matthew 7:15-27; 13:24-30, 36-53.
John 4:43—5:18; 21. Acts 18. II Timothy 2:1-15.

Labor Day Litany

Leader: For Thy deliverance of all who are overworked,
or burdened or enslaved, for Thy protection of all whose
labor brings them into danger, for Thy comfort of those
whose toil is unpleasant or monotonous, or without joy,

Response: We beseech Thee, O Lord.

Leader: For Thy remembrance of all who are out of
work, for Thy mercy upon those who are driven to rebel-
lion or despair,

Response: We beseech Thee, O Lord.

Leader: For those who are careless, for those who are unconcerned of the conditions under which others live,

Response: We beseech Thee, O Lord.

Leader: For the ending of industrial strife, for the establishment of true fellowship among men, for the coming of Thy Kingdom,

Response: O Lord, hear us, and answer us according to Thy will in Christ. Amen.

Pastor's Labor Day Prayer

Among all Thy gifts to us, O God, on this Labor Day Sunday we would not be ungrateful for our daily work, and the joy and satisfaction that is ours when we give honest labor and loving service. Make us to feel the sense of being co-workers with Thee. Forgive those who labor with lazy complacency, and for selfish purposes. Guard the labor leaders from lust for personal power and hasten the day when unprincipled men shall be eliminated from positions of authority. Unite in service for the common good both employer and employees, masters and servants, rich and poor. Keep us, Father, from trivialities that we may recognize the great causes that await our energy and intelligence. Amen.

WORLD ORDER SUNDAY

Call to Worship

God was in Christ reconciling the world to himself . . . and entrusting to us the message of reconciliation. So we are ambassadors for Christ, God making his appeal through us. . . . How beautiful upon the mountains are the feet of him who brings good tidings, who publishes peace, who brings good tidings of good, who publishes salvation (*II Corinthians 5:19, 20; Isaiah 52:7*).

Invocation

Almighty God, from whom all thoughts of truth and peace proceed: Kindle, we pray Thee, in the hearts of all men the true love of peace, and guide with Thy pure and peaceable wisdom those who take counsel for the nations of the earth; that in tranquility Thy Kingdom may go forward, till the earth is filled with the knowledge of Thy love; through Jesus Christ our Lord. Amen.[20]

Scripture Lessons

Psalms: 46; 67.
Old Testament: Isaiah 2:1-5; 11:1-10; 41:9-14, 17-20.
New Testament: Matthew 26:47-52. John 18:36. Hebrews 12:1-29. James 3:13-18; 4:1-10.

World Order Litany

Leader: O Father of all men, we pray for the realization of brotherhood among the nations, a brotherhood rooted in Thy Fatherhood. May each nation find its own freedom in giving itself to world comradeship, and in rendering service to the good of all.

Response: Hear our prayer, O Lord.

Leader: Unite all peoples of the world in an order of peace. Destroy the influences which create bitterness and division. Purge diplomacy and commerce of all that is base and mean, and hasten the day when nation shall not lift up sword against nation, nor learn war any more.

Response: Hear our prayer, O Lord.

Leader: O Thou whose service is perfect freedom, loosen, we beseech Thee, the fetters of the hindered races of the earth; deliver them from galling bonds and heal their wounds. May their rights and liberties be protected by the great nations of mankind; and grant that each tribe and people, freed by justice to do justly, and by mercy to be merciful, may find its soul in the unity of love, and do its part in Thy world family.

Response: Hear our prayer, O Lord.

Leader: Save the world from unholy ambition, from the lust of power, and from armed enmity among the nations; and prosper those who seek to check the beginnings of discord and to spread the message of good will.

Response: Hear our prayer, O Lord.[21]

Pastor's World Order Prayer

O God, who hast made of one blood all nations of men to dwell on the face of the earth, who didst send the Prince of Peace to show us how to live in harmony: Forgive our personal involvement and the seeds of disorder, war, enmity, and selfishness which are in our own hearts.

Surely, Lord, Thou dost grieve over the plight of our world. Surely, the impoverished, thirsting, hungering masses fill Thy heart with despair. Surely Thou dost yearn for a change in the cruel, ruthless, selfish policies which dominate our nations. Surely Thou dost want a demonstration of Thy Spirit and Thy ways in order that good might dispel evil.

Grant us, then, this day, renewed concern. May we see others as they are seen through the tender eyes of Christ. Give us disturbing sympathy for innocent victims of the world's injustices. Displace our selfish smugness with involvement in the world's pain.

O Lord, we need Thy help to do something about the world's true problems, which are our own—the problem of lying which we call propaganda, the problem of selfishness which we call security, the problem of greed which we call profit, the problem of lust masquerading as love.

O Lord, help us to build the instruments of peace in service agencies, courts, covenants, and parliaments. Grant us the wisdom to build a warless world. Teach us to control our economic life, and to unite all peace-loving men in opposition to war. Thus, may Thy Kingdom come on earth as it is in heaven. Amen.

THANKSGIVING SUNDAY

Call to Worship

O give thanks to the Lord, for he is good, for his steadfast love endures for ever (*Psalm 136:1*).

Invocation

Source of all we see and all that we do not see, by whose goodness we have been created, by whose bounty we are sustained, and by whose love we are being redeemed: Thou art worthy of a greater praise than our lips can utter. Accept then, our expressions of thankfulness in service, offering, and dedication, through Jesus Christ. Amen.

Scripture Lessons

Psalms: 65:1, 2, 9-13; 100; 107:31-43; 147; 150.
Old Testament: Deuteronomy 8; 26:1-11; 28:1-14. Isaiah 12. Ezekiel 34:22-31.
New Testament: Matthew 6. Luke 12:13-34; 17:11-19. Acts 14:8-17. Philippians 4. I Thessalonians 4:9—5:28. James 1.

Thanksgiving Litany

Leader: O God, our Father, fountain of all goodness, who hast been gracious to us through all the years of our life: We give Thee thanks for Thy lovingkindness which hath filled our days and brought us to this time and place.

Response: We praise Thy holy name, O Lord.

Leader: Thou hast given us life and reason, and set us in the world which is full of Thy glory. Thou hast comforted us with kindred and friends, and ministered to us through the hands and minds of our fellows.

Response: We praise Thy holy name, O Lord.

Leader: Thou hast set in our hearts a hunger for Thee, and given us Thy peace. Thou hast redeemed us and called us to a high calling in Christ Jesus. Thou hast given us a place in the fellowship of Thy Spirit and the witness of Thy Church.

Response: We praise Thy holy name, O Lord.

Leader: In darkness Thou hast been our light, in adversity and temptation a rock of strength, in our joys the very spirit of joy, in our labors the all-sufficient reward.

Response: We praise Thy holy name, O Lord.

Leader: Thou hast remembered us when we have forgotten Thee, followed us even when we fled from Thee, met us with forgiveness when we turned back to Thee. For all Thy longsuffering and the abundance of Thy grace,

Response: We praise Thy holy name, O Lord.[22]

Pastor's Thanksgiving Prayer

We thank Thee, our Father, for life and love, for the mystery and majesty of existence, for the world of beauty which surrounds us and for the miracle of our conscious life by which we behold the wonders of the universe.

We thank Thee for the glimpses of nobility in human life which redeem it from sordidness and reassure us that Thine image is in the heart of man. We are grateful for the ties which bind us to our fellow men; for the common toil in industry and marts of trade; for our joint inheritance as citizens of this nation; for traditions and customs hallowed by age through which our passions are ordered and channeled; for the love of beauty and truth and goodness by which we transcend the chasms of race and nation; for the faith of our fathers by which we claim kinship with the past and gain strength for the present; for the love of dear ones in our homes and for the enlarging responsibilities and sobering duties of our family life; for the serenity of old people who redeem us of fretfulness and for the faith and courage of youth through which we are saved from sloth.

We are unworthy of the rich inheritances of our common life. We confess that we have profaned the temple of this life by our selfishness and heedlessness. We have sought to gain advantage of our brothers who are bound together with us by many different ties. Have mercy upon us that we may express our gratitude for Thy many mercies by contrition for our sins and that we may prove our repentance by lives dedicated more fully to Thee and to the common good, through Jesus Christ our Lord. Amen.[23]

OTHER SPECIAL OCCASIONS MATERIAL

ORDINATION OF A MINISTER

A Charge to Newly Ordained Minister

My Brother: You have been ordained to the office of the holy Ministry . . . and have been commissioned to preach the Word, to administer the sacraments, and to perform those other duties appointed by the Church. I now charge you, in the name of the Lord Jesus, the great head of the Church, to be faithful in this your high calling. I exhort you, in the name of our Lord Jesus Christ, that you have in remembrance into how high a dignity, and to how weighty an office, you have been set apart; that is to say, to be a messenger, watchman, and steward of the Lord; to teach and admonish, to feed and provide for the Lord's flock; to seek for Christ's sheep that are dispersed abroad, and for His children who are in the midst of this evil world, that they may be saved through Jesus Christ for ever.

Have always, therefore, in remembrance how great a treasure is committed to your charge, for they are the sheep of Christ, for which He shed His blood. The Church and congregation which you must serve is His Body. And if it shall happen that the same Church, or any member thereof, do take any hurt or hindrance by reason of your negligence, you know the greatness of the fault. Wherefore, consider with yourself the end of the ministry toward the children of God, toward the Church, the Body of Christ; and never cease your labor, your care, and diligence until you have done all that lieth in you to bring all such as are or shall be committed to your charge unto agreement in the faith and knowledge of God.

Forasmuch then as your office is both of so great excellency and of so great difficulty, with great care and study you ought to apply yourself, as well to show yourself dutiful and thankful unto the Lord who hath placed you in so high a dignity; as also to beware that you neither yourself offend nor be occasion that others offend. Howbeit, you cannot have a mind and will thereto of yourself;

for the will and ability are given of God alone; therefore you ought, and have need, to pray earnestly for His Holy Spirit. And seeing that you cannot by any other means compass the doing of so weighty a work, pertaining to the salvation of man, but with doctrine and exhortation taken out of the Holy Scriptures, and with a life agreeable to the same, consider how studious you ought to be in reading and learning the Scriptures.

We have good hope that you have well weighed these things long before this time; and that you have clearly determined by God's grace to give yourself to this holy Ministry, whereunto it hath pleased God to call you; so that you will apply yourself wholly to this one thing, and draw all your cares and studies this way; and that you will continually pray to God the Father, by the meditation of our only Saviour Jesus Christ, for the heavenly assistance of the Holy Spirit; that, by daily reading and weighing the Scriptures, you may wax riper and stronger in your ministry; and that you may so endeavor yourself, from time to time, to sanctify the lives of yourself and others, and to fashion them after the rule and doctrine of Christ, that you may be a wholesome and godly example and pattern for the people to follow.

We commend you to God, and to the Word of His grace, which is able to build you up and to give you an inheritance among all them which are sanctified; through Jesus Christ our Lord. Amen.[24]

Ordination Prayer for a Christian Minister

God and Father of mankind, who hast blessed the world with salvation in Christ, who hast given birth to the Church, and age after age hast called men to be missionaries, teachers, pastors, and evangelists: We thank Thee that

Thou hast called this young man to this holy office. We thank Thee for the influences which have led him to this day—the Christ that inspired him, his family which encouraged him, the church that has nurtured him, the ministers and friends who have challenged him.

As he is set apart for Thy holy work, our Father, arm him with a strong body, an alert and sound mind, and a genuine Christian spirit. Grant him a growing knowledge of Thee, courage to rebuke sin in its every manifestation, and an understanding of people. Enrich him with good judgment, wholesome humor, kindly insight, gracious utterance and unflagging zeal. Endow him with patience, sincerity, tolerance, and generosity that through his efforts souls may be brought to the feet of Christ, hearts may be filled with a new song, evil may be stamped out by right, and the world made a better place.

When his serving days are over, may he receive the crown of life, which is above every reward, and Thy commendation, "Well done, good and faithful servant, enter into the joy of thy Lord," in whose name we pray. Amen.

INSTALLATION OF OFFICERS

A Covenant of Fidelity: (*It may be asked of those being installed.*) Do you each accept the office to which you have been elected (or appointed), and do you promise, the Lord being your helper, faithfully to fulfill its duties?

The Response: (*in unison*) I do.

A Covenant of the Older Officers: (*Officers whose terms have not expired should stand.*) Do you gladly receive these as fellow officers serving with you in their varied responsibilities, covenanting to work together as laborers with God? If so, please indicate your willingness by saying in unison, I do.

The Response: (*in unison*) I do.

A Covenant by the Congregation (or Group): Will you pledge your eager support to the work of God in this congregation (or organization) under the leadership of these, your fellow members who have been selected to serve (or, whom you have elected to office), and will you renew your vows of fidelity by standing and engaging with me in a common covenant?

The Response: (*in unison*) We will.

The Covenant: (*in unison*) Affirming our membership in the holy church throughout all the world, and our fellowship in this congregation with those who have obtained a like precious faith, we renew our vows of fidelity to our Lord Jesus Christ, and solemnly covenant and promise:

That we will walk together in brotherly love, as is becoming in members of a Christian church; that we will not forsake the assembling of ourselves together; that we will endeavor to bring up such as may at any time be under our care, in the nurture and admonition of the Lord, and by a pure and holy example, to win our kindred and acquaintances to the Saviour, to holiness, and to eternal life; that we will regularly support the work of the church by systematic contributions of money.

The Installation Prayer: Set apart, O Lord, these Thy servants, to the work whereunto they have been called by the voice of the church. Endue them plenteously with heavenly wisdom. Grant them Thy grace, that they may be good men, full of the Holy Spirit and of faith, ruling in the fear of God. Give them that favor and influence with the people which come from following Christ. So fill them with His Spirit that they may lead this congregation (or people) in His service. Make them faithful unto death, and when the Chief Shepherd shall appear, may they receive a crown of glory that fadeth not away. Amen.

Opening Sentence

Behold, I stand at the door and knock; if any one hears my voice and opens the door, I will come in (*Revelation 3:20*).

Invocation

Eternal God, Father of all: We recognize Thee as the source and giver of the love which draws families together. We pray that Thou wilt be present in this home, that Thy love may enrich its fellowship, Thy wisdom be its guide, Thy truth its light, and Thy peace its benediction, through Jesus Christ, our Lord. Amen.

A Beatitude for the Family

> Happy is the family that has a true home built by loyal hearts,
> For home is not a dwelling but a living fellowship,
> In love and understanding.
> And happy is the family whose members find a deeper unity
> In sharing truth and beauty and devotion to the good.
> Their love shall be an altar fire
> Burning in the temple of the Highest.

Scripture Reading

A new commandment I give to you, that you love one another; even as I have loved you, that you also love one another. By this all men will know that you are my disciples, if you have love for one another (*John 13:34, 35*).

Love is patient and kind; love is not jealous or boastful;

it is not arrogant or rude. Love does not insist on its own way; it is not irritable or resentful; it does not rejoice at wrong, but rejoices in the right. Love bears all things, believes all things, hopes all things, endures all things (*I Corinthians 13:4-7*).

Dedication and Candle-lighting Ceremony

(*Parts may be adapted and assigned to various members of the family.*)

We dedicate this home to love and understanding. May its joys and sorrows be shared and the individuality of each member appreciated. We light a candle to *Family Love*.

We dedicate this home to work and leisure. May it have gaiety and high fellowship, with kindness in its voices and laughter ringing within its walls. We light a candle to *Happiness*.

We dedicate this home to a friendly life. May its doors open in hospitality and its windows look out with kindness toward other homes. We light a candle to *Friendship*.

We dedicate this home to cooperation. May its duties be performed in love, its furnishings bear witness that the work of others ministers to our comfort, and its table remind us that God works with us for the supply of our daily needs. We light a candle to *Cooperation*.

We dedicate this home to the appreciation of all things good and true. May the books bring wisdom, the pictures symbolize things beautiful, and the music bring joy and inspiration. We light a candle to *Appreciation*.

We dedicate the time and talents of those who will live here to serve our generation and to help build a world in which every family may have a home of comfort and fellowship. We light a candle to *Christian Service*.

We dedicate this home as a unit in the Church universal, an instrument of the Kingdom of God, a place for worship and Christian training and a threshold to the life eternal. We light a candle to *Spiritual Enrichment*.

As the flames point upward, so our thoughts rise in gratitude to God for this home, and in prayer for His blessing upon it.[25]

Prayer of Dedication

Lord, bless this dwelling, not for any richness of material nor beauty of design, not for grace of furnishing nor for loveliness of site. For all these we thank Thee. But especially bless this house because here is home; home for son in years of grave decision; home for daughter in springtime of her life; home for her who weaves the fabric of the family, the repeated tasks of days and nights; home for him who must please and fight and labor to protect, enrich, to train and fit the young; refuge for hard-pressed spirit and pain-filled body; castle behind whose walls all may rest to go out refreshed to fresh achievement.

Let doors be wide enough to welcome all friendly spirits, the table have bread for all hungry mouths, the beds hospitable to the weary, the books appraising of the harvest of the spirit, a home friendly and kind to every neighbor. Here let all gossip cease, all unworthy blame be left unspoken; here may gaiety and seriousness alternate to meet the total needs of life. Here let steadiness replace nervous haste, a sense of mission relieve nagging lust for power. Here let the old, quaint, true, everlasting gospel embrace a family in undying bonds of love, through Jesus Christ, our Lord. Amen.[26]

Solo or Reading

> Bless this house, O Lord, we pray,
> Make it safe by night and day;
> Bless these walls so firm and stout;
> Keeping want and trouble out;
> Bless the roof and chimney tall,
> Let Thy peace lie over all;
> Bless this door that it may prove
> Ever open to joy and love.
> Bless these windows shining bright,
> Letting in God's heavenly light;
> Bless the hearth a-blazing there;
> With smoke ascending like a prayer;
> Bless the folk who dwell within,
> Keep them pure and free from sin;
> Bless us all that we may be,
> Fit, O Lord, to dwell with Thee.[27]
>   —Helen Taylor

Benediction

The Lord bless you and keep you, the Lord make His face to shine upon you and be gracious unto you, the Lord lift up His countenance upon you, and give you peace, both now and for ever. Amen.

PASTORAL PRAYER AT BEGINNING OF PASTORATE

Almighty God, whose providence has led us into this pastoral relationship, we thank Thee for this inexpressible privilege of being Thy servants. May Thy Holy Spirit bless our ministry together as we grow and serve.

Thou, O Lord, hast made me Thy spiritual shepherd of this people. Grant me humility in face of the task. May their well-being be my chief concern. Fill my heart with a love for each one. Give me the knowledge of how to serve them spiritually in all their varied circumstances. O Lord, help me to be faithful in study, unflagging in prayer, blameless in living, and unselfish in service that I may be Thy prophet in such a confused time and may direct minds and hearts into Thy presence. Grant me patience to work out the full potential of this opportunity, faith in the leadership of this congregation, an evangelistic spirit to seek the least and lost, and a wisdom to know the issues of this day.

O Lord, bless this people with harmony. May they forget the successes and failures of the past that creep into the present to hinder the future. Forgive, merciful God, the grudges and resentments of yesteryears that unfit us for facing today. Spare us from smallness of vision, shallowness of dedication, half-committed stewardship, and bitterness of unguarded moments. Help us to examine anew Thy saving grace, to look again through Thine eyes, to feel the compulsion of Thy challenge, and to be stirred as never before by the urgency of our task in building Thy Kingdom on earth as it is in heaven. To Thee, O Christ, we dedicate ourselves. Amen.

PASTORAL PRAYER AT CONCLUSION OF PASTORATE

O God, the shepherd of Thy people through their earthly wanderings, who dost neither slumber nor sleep: We bow before Thee as sheep of Thy pasture. Beside the still waters, we now wait with Thee. We know not what the future has of "marvel or surprise," of green pastures or of valleys of dark shadows; whatever it be, be Thou our strength and shield.

We thank Thee for the shared joys, successes, and friendships that have blessed this pastoral relationship. We remember in gratitude the bright hours of faith, the many examples of sacrifice, the depth of love demonstrated, the spiritual recoveries made, and the high moments when Thy

Holy Spirit glowed within. Bless this congregation with harmony, rekindle its vision, and commit it anew to Thy mission.

Good Shepherd, fold us safely in Thy love lest we be overtaken by storm, or lost in darkness, or in carelessness or curiosity wander from Thy care. Save us from following the clamor of the world. May we not forget that poverty and riches are of the spirit.

When age and infirmity overtake us, may we be found thankful for life and time's golden memories that are sweet and good. At eventide, when life's lamp is burning low, may we lie down safely in Thine eternal fold, to the glory of Jesus Christ in whom there is no separation. Amen.

PASTOR'S PRAYER AT A FAMILY REUNION

O Thou, Heavenly Father of us all, by whose kind providence we have been privileged to meet here: We express orally the thanks we feel inwardly, and acknowledge all that Thy presence has meant to this family.

We thank Thee for the dear, new lives who have been born into these families, and those who have married into it. We are thankful for the children who have grown to manhood and womanhood. Guard them from life's perils. Keep them true to the pledge of their youth to serve humanity, and support them with the "faith of their fathers living still."

We recall with tenderness our dear ones who have departed from us, and who are now at home with Thee. We acknowledge our indebtedness to those who have contributed so much to our lives. Heaven has taken on a warmer glow since they entered into that home.

We would pray for all the families of the earth and for the greater family in which we all share as Thy children.

Break through the barriers that separate us, and hasten the day when the human family shall be one in Thee, through Jesus Christ our Lord. Amen.

PASTOR'S EVANGELISTIC PRAYER

O God of us all, whose wisdom is beyond the reaches of our minds, whose mercy is wider than our wanderings, and whose redeeming love is deeper than our sins: We bow in humility before Thee. By Thy goodness our souls are fed. By Thy truth our minds are enlightened. By Thy Son, Jesus Christ, we have forgiveness and life abundant.

O Lord, we confess that too much we have lived as if there were no God. We have followed our own way as if Jesus had never lived. We have dressed ourselves up outwardly without adorning ourselves inwardly. We have built fine mansions in which to live, but have not bothered to learn how to live. We have pursued the things that perish in the grasping, and have been indifferent to those treasures of the spirit in which there is eternal security. We have been serious over the trivial and trivial over the serious. O God, have mercy upon us, and forgive us.

O Lord God, may some insight pierce through our rationalizations to revive our hunger for Thee. Cause the music of the gospel to stir the lost chords of our souls that a new song may be sung in our hearts. May Thy Holy Spirit burn through the sham of our excuses, melting away false barriers, rekindling love that has grown cold, and allowing the best in each one to have its way. May Jesus Christ and His church have a more compelling claim upon our lives than ever before. Since we know not what a day may bring forth, and that the hour for obeying and serving Thee is present, give us the courage to yield to Jesus Christ today. Amen.

INVOCATIONS FOR COMMUNITY OCCASIONS

FOR AN ATHLETIC CONTEST

O Thou who didst wonderfully create us with bodies of potential skill, and minds that enjoy achievement: We pause in gratitude to acknowledge the spiritual benefits of competitive athletics in teaching teamwork, discipline, unselfishness, cooperation, fairness, and obedience to rules. Bless the participants in this contest with clean sportsmanship, so that those who lose may do so without alibi and with such generosity that they will thus be winning, and those who win without vain boasting, but with humility that all will be better prepared for the great game of life in obedience to our Divine Manager. Amen.

FOR A SERVICE COMMITTEE MEETING

O God, in whose name we are met, and for whose Kingdom of Truth and Justice we have dedicated ourselves: We bow in humility as a service committee recognizing that our ardor is but a feeble shadow of Thy concern, our wisdom is but a fraction of Thine understanding, and our power is meager without Thine. As we reflect upon Thee, we pray that Thou wilt deepen our concern, enlarge our understanding, and imbue us with power for the task at hand. For the sake of Jesus Christ and His Kingdom. Amen.

FOR A PUBLIC SCHOOL ASSEMBLY

Thou, fountain of all wisdom, author of all truth, who has created us with minds to learn Thy thoughts, and bodies to serve Thy ways: Bless these young people with proper friendship, careful counsel, stimulating teachers, noble examples, and serious endeavors that they might learn that worth knowing, to love that worth loving, and to do that worth doing, thus to please Thee, unto whom all must give account through Jesus Christ our Lord. Amen.

FOR A UNION CHURCH MEETING

Divine Spirit of Love, in whom there is harmony and perfect concord, and who art the Heavenly Father of us all: We thank Thee for the bonds of brotherly affection, the embrace of Christian charity, for the unanimity of mind, and the common challenge of Jesus Christ, which transcends our differences and brings us to this expression of oneness, after Thy Divine Nature in Jesus Christ. Amen.

FOR A MINISTERIAL ASSOCIATION MEETING

Thou Eternal Shepherd of Thy sheep, who hast chosen us to be under-shepherds: We humble ourselves before Thee, mindful of a task too great for us alone, cognizant of the needs of the community we serve, feeling the support of this fraternal fellowship, the power of the gospel of Christ, and praying for new insights into Thy will and renewed strength for Thy work. Forbid that we should get in Thy way. Save us from the perils of temptation. Make us more effective channels of Thy Spirit. Unite us in harmonious endeavor. And bless our several efforts that Thy glory may be seen and Thy saving ways known to all men through Jesus Christ, whose we are and whom we serve. Amen.

FOR A POLITICAL RALLY

For the democratic principle by which we can all participate in the ordering of our community, state, and national life, we pause in gratitude before Thee. Grant that we might be concerned enough to be informed, wise enough to choose leaders of integrity and ability, American enough to rise above party loyalty, and responsible enough to vote for the sake of justice as we know it in Thee. Amen.

FOR A CIVIC CLUB MEETING

Almighty God: We are assembled here as workmen from many businesses, various faiths, and divergent views, to lift up our thoughts of gratitude, to share our common interests and problems, and to make this community in particular and the world in general a better place for the dwelling of Thy children. To these purposes we now commit ourselves. Amen.

FOR THE CHAMBER OF COMMERCE MEETING

Thou who didst from the beginning walk with man in the cool of the day, come to commune with us now. We stand at attention before Thee, O God, in gratitude for our unlimited blessings, not the least of which is the freedom we enjoy, the privilege of living in this beautiful city and this association.

Save us from misuse of freedom without restraint; help us as leaders to seek not the good of any faction, but of all citizens, ever sustained with a high vision of righteousness. Guide our mayor and city officers to develop our community in Thy ways, for Thy name's sake. Amen.

FOR A PATRIOTIC OCCASION

O Lord of history, through whose power men won liberty, and by whose justice they beheld the vision of a righteous nation, and by whose will they laid down their lives to purchase it: We are not unmindful of the heritage which is ours, not of our deserving but by Thy providence, and bought with diligence, scholarship, and sacrifice. Help us to be worthy to stand in this place in the time allotted to us, and with steadfast courage and unwavering hope to fulfill the tasks which Thy will demands be done. Amen.

Notes

SECTION I

1. Willett and Morrison, *The Daily Altar* (New York, Harper & Brothers, 1918), p. 155.
2. Adapted from St. Francis of Assisi.

SECTION II

1. Ralph W. Sockman, *The Higher Happiness* (Nashville: Abingdon Press, 1950), p. 149.
2. Author unknown.
3. *The Book of Common Prayer,* p. 67.
4. William Angus Knight, *Prayers Ancient and Modern* (London: J. M. Dent Publishers, used by permission of the E. P. Dutton Company, New York).

SECTION III

1. James DeForest Murch, *A Christian Minister's Manual* (Cincinnati: Standard Publishing, 1937), p. 56.

SECTION IV

1. Based on *The Book of Common Prayer.*
2. Source unknown. Used frequently at the International Convention of Christian Churches (Disciples of Christ).
3. Author unknown.
4. Author unknown, *Minister's Manual,* ed. Rev. M. K. W. Heicher (New York: Harper & Brothers, 1960), pp. 43-44.
5. Roderick Bethune, *Minister's Manual,* ed. Rev. M. K. W. Heicher, *op. cit.,* p. 44.
6. George Pease, *The Elder at the Lord's Table,* ed. Thomas Toler (St. Louis: Christian Board of Publication, 1954), p. 76. Used by permission.
7. John Oxenham, "No East or West," *Bees in Amber* (Westwood, New Jersey: Fleming H. Revell Company, 1959), p. 61.

SECTION V

1. *The Book of Worship for Church and Home* (New York: The Methodist Publishing House, 1944, 1945), pp. 390-391.

SECTION VI

1. R. C. Cave, *A Manual for Ministers* (Cincinnati: Standard Publishing Company), pp. 63-68.
2. *The Book of Common Prayer (1549),* pp. 300-304.
3. *A Book of Worship for Free Churches* (New York: Oxford University Press, 1948), pp. 157-159. Copyright 1948 by The Board of Home Missions of the Congregational and Christian Churches. All rights reserved.

SECTION VII

1. Author unknown.
2. Rev. Charles E. Hannan, Associate Minister, First Christian Church, San Angelo, Texas.
3. Kahlil Gibran, *The Prophet* (New York: Alfred A. Knopf, 1923), pp. 21-22.

SECTION VIII

1. Dr. G. Edwin Osborn, *Christian Worship: A Service Book* (St. Louis: Christian Board of Publication, 1953), p. 93. Used by permission.
2. Robert E. Chiles, "The Lord Is My Shepherd," *Pulpit Digest,* January, 1960, pp. 55-56. Copyright 1959 by the Pulpit Digest Publishing Company.
3. John Henry Newman.

SECTION IX

1. Edmund H. Babbitt, *Strength for Hospital Days* (Chicago: Board of Hospitals and Homes of The Methodist Church, 1946), p. 1.
2. Samuel F. Pugh, *When You Are a Hospital Patient* (Indianapolis: Department of Church Development and Evangelism of the United Christian Missionary Society), p. 10.
3. Edmund H. Babbitt, *op. cit.,* p. 2.
4. Based on Romans 8:28.

5. Samuel F. Pugh, *op. cit.,* p. 14.

6. Armin Frederick Bahnsen, *My Companion for Quiet Hours* (Cleveland: Church World Press, Inc.), pp. 15-16.

7. Katherine Lee Bates, *My Companion for Quiet Hours,* Armin Frederick Bahnsen, *op. cit.,* p. 13.

8. Edmund H. Babbitt, *op. cit.,* p. 6.

9. James DeForest Murch, *A Christian Minister's Manual, op. cit.,* p. 35.

10. Richard C. Cabot and Russell L. Dicks, *The Art of Ministering to the Sick* (New York: The Macmillan Company, 1936), p. 224.

11. *Ibid.,* p. 225.

12. *Ibid.,* p. 226.

13. *Ibid.,* p. 227.

14. *Ibid.,* p. 230.

15. *Ibid.,* p. 229.

16. *Ibid.,* p. 226.

17. From *The Book of Common Prayer* of the Church of Ireland (altered).

18. Cabot and Dicks, *op. cit.,* p. 222.

19. *Ibid.,* p. 231.

SECTION X

1. Wallace Petty, *Minister's Service Book,* ed. James Dalton Morrison (New York: Harper & Brothers, 1937).

2. John Wallace Suter, *Worship Resources,* ed. Charles L. Wallis (New York: Harper & Brothers, 1954), p. 71.

3. Author unknown, *Worship Resources,* ed. Charles L. Wallis, *op. cit.,* p. 72.

4. Boynton Merrill, *Arrows of Light* (New York: Harper & Brothers, 1935).

5. *Divine Worship* (London: Epworth Press, 1935).

6. *A Book of Worship for Free Churches, op. cit.,* p. 372.

7. William E. Orchard, *Worship Resources,* ed. Charles L. Wallis, *op. cit.,* p. 99.

8. William E. Orchard, *The Order of Divine Service for Public Worship* (London: Oxford University Press, 1925), p. 73.

9. Richard K. Morton, *Worship Resources,* ed. Charles L. Wallis, *op. cit.,* p. 99.

10. William E. Orchard, *The Temple—A Book of Prayers* (London: J. M. Dent and Sons, 1913), p. 97.

11. Produced by National Council of Churches of Christ, *Worship Resources,* ed. Charles L. Wallis, *op. cit.,* p. 137.

12. Wilbur P. Thirkfield and Oliver Huckel, *Church Worship Book* (Boston: Sidney A. Weston, 1931), p. 184.

13. George H. Russell, *Intercession Services* (Boston: Pilgrim Press, 1930).

14. Armin C. Oldsen, *Worship Resources,* ed. Charles L. Wallis, *op. cit.,* p. 279.

15. John Hunter, *Divine Service for Public Worship* (New York: E. P. Dutton & Co., Inc.).

16. Author unknown, *Worship Resources,* ed. Charles L. Wallis, *op. cit.,* p. 385.

17. Morgan Phelps Noyes, *Prayers for Services* (New York: Charles Scribner's Sons, 1945), p. 191.

18. *The Book of Common Prayer,* p. 263.

19. Leslie D. Weatherhead, *Pulpit Digest,* July, 1952.

20. Francis Paget, *Worship Resources,* ed. Charles L. Wallis, *op. cit.,* p. 216.

21. George H. Russell, *Intercession Services, op. cit.*

22. *The Book of Worship for Church and Home* (New York: The Methodist Publishing House, 1944, 1945), p. 41.

23. Reinhold Niebuhr, *Worship Resources,* ed. Charles L. Wallis, *op. cit.,* p. 346.

24. *The Book of Common Worship* (Philadelphia: Board of Christian Education of Presbyterian Church USA, 1946), pp. 231-233.

25. Adaptation of service prepared by Commission on Marriage and the Home of the National Council of Churches of Christ of America.

26. George Stewart, *A Face to the Sky* (New York: Association Press by International Council of YMCA, 1940), p. 11.

27. Boosey and Hawks, Inc., New York.